THE COLLECTED WRI

VOLUME IX

GOD'S AMAZING
SALVATION

VOLUME 1

JACK COTTRELL

THE CHRISTIAN RESTORATION ASSOCIATION

TABLE OF CONTENTS

PREFACE

When I was sorting out all the smaller writings I have produced over the decades, I was a bit surprised at how many of them fall under the subject of salvation. When measured by volume, there is almost twice as much material on this subject as on any of the other subjects. This means that there will be two volumes under the title, *God's Amazing Salvation*.

I guess I should not have been surprised at all, since salvation is probably the subject that lies closer to our hearts than the others. Also, it has been the subject of a great many of the questions that have come to me by my Facebook friends, and therefore the subject of many of the short essays that have appeared on my website (www.jackcottrell.com) and in my *Restoration Herald* column, "Ask the Professor."

Salvation has also been the main focus of my theological study and teaching for my entire career. When I was constructing the theological curriculum for the fledgling Cincinnati Bible Seminary graduate school (I began teaching in 1967), I designed a "Basic Theology" course which would be required of all students. Since it was only three credit hours, I could not cover all the subjects usually included in Systematic Theology; so I limited it to the doctrines of man, sin, and salvation.

My main efforts in the study of salvation, however, have been directed to one single aspect of this topic, namely, the doctrine of grace. At the request of our graduate dean, Dr. Lewis Foster, in my first semester of teaching I offered a course called "New Testament Theology." I asked Dr. Foster what he wanted me to cover in that course. He said, "Whatever you think best." (Good answer!) I decided to begin to unfold the main fountain of grace in the New Testament, the Book of Romans. I taught this course every year, but after a year or two I changed the name to "The Doctrine of Grace." I probably taught that course at least 70 times over the years.

Grace is a subject that never received any special attention in the whole history of the Restoration Movement. I am sorry to say that I learned almost nothing about it from my childhood preachers or during my five years of full-time study at CBS (1955-1960). It began to especially impress itself upon my mind and heart during my three years at Westminster Theological Seminary (1962-1965). This was not so much the result of my Calvinist teachers there, as it was the result of being exposed to the teachings of the Protestant Reformers, especially Martin Luther. This exposure continued in my two years at Princeton Theological Seminary (1965-1967).

When I returned to CBS and began to teach especially what Paul says about grace in Romans, it was so new and different from what most had ever heard that I was sometimes accused of teaching the Calvinism I had learned at Westminster. (Believe me, there is a world of difference between Calvinism and Biblical grace as I understand it!) Anyway, I was not hindered from my mission of giving the Restoration Plea a distinctive grace flavor. After all, it was good for Paul and Silas, and it's good enough for me!

Still, there were hurdles to overcome, one of which stands out in my mind. When I teach about the content of salvation, I usually break it down into a "double cure," but the second part of it has two separate aspects of salvation. Thus salvation consists of these three elements: justification, regeneration, and sanctification. Here we are focusing on regeneration. I believe and teach that regeneration (i.e., the new birth, spiritual resurrection) is not something *we* do, but something the Holy Spirit does *to us*, in the moment of baptism. One day early in my years of teaching, I was "invited" to a meeting in the president's office. There sat the President, Harvey Bream, and three of our most prestigious professors: two from the college—George Mark Elliott and Sherwood Smith, and one from the graduate school—Harold Ford. The chairman of our board, Wayne Smith, was also there.

The three professors were accusing me of teaching Calvinism, because I was teaching that the Holy Spirit regenerates us by working *directly* on the hearts of sinners. Their own view was one frequently taught in the Restoration Movement, namely, that the change called regeneration is the change that takes place in the sinner's heart before baptism as the result of one's own faith and repentance. In effect, the sinner regenerates himself; the Spirit works only indirectly, through the Word. I did my best to explain the difference between what I was teaching on the one hand, and both of the false views—theirs and Calvinism's—on the other hand. In the end I satisfied the president and the chairman of the board enough so that my tenure at CBS did not come to an end at that time. I went back to my office and wept for quite a while, though.

Looking back on my nearly 50 years of teaching and writing on grace, I can truly say that it has been the most satisfying and rewarding experience of my life. I do not know how many times I have had a student tell me after taking my course on grace, "That course has changed my life," or "That course has changed my ministry." Praise God!

About ten years ago I decided to put the contents of my grace course into book form, so in 2009 College Press published *Set Free! What the Bible Says About Grace* (401 pages). Also, my book on systematic theology, *The Faith Once for All* (College Press, 2002) has six chapters on salvation themes, including chapter 16, "Salvation: By Law or by Grace?"

This volume includes only about one-half of the items on salvation; see volume II for the rest. In this one, most of the selections are on grace themes. Section One begins with three sermons on salvation, the last one of which ("The Robe of Righteousness") summarizes what it means to be saved by grace. It is based on Isaiah 61:10. I have preached it over 50 times.

The next section is mostly about the message of Romans 1-8. The two summaries of these Romans chapters were written about 40 years apart. There is also a small piece on Galatians, too.

Section three has entries that specifically discuss grace. You will notice references to *law* and grace. My main theme for grace is taken from Paul's statement in Romans 6:14, "You are not under law, but under grace." These are the two options between which we must choose to try to be right with God. Paul's point is that *only* the grace option can be successful. I think all of these essays will be very helpful to you.

Section four focuses on what I believe is the heart of salvation and the heart of grace, the doctrine of *justification by faith*. We in the Restoration Movement have put a lot of emphasis on forgiveness of sins, but somehow have mostly failed to connect that with justification. Actually, justification and forgiveness are the same thing, contrary to what the Protestant world usually teaches. Also, we Restorationists have shied away from the grand teaching of justification by faith, because we associate that with Calvinism and Zwinglianism (i.e., "faith-onlyism"). That is sad, because justification by faith is the most amazing and joyful part of grace. We and the rest of the Christian world need to see that justification *by faith* (as the *means* of receiving salvation) is fully consistent with forgiveness or justification *in baptism* (as the *time* of receiving salvation—Colossians 2:12).

Also section four has a few things related to our common misunderstanding of 1 John 1:9. Our misunderstanding here is one of the main reasons why we have had difficulty being confident and assured of our salvation status before God. We need to change the way we explain this text.

Section Five is one item, "The Christian World View." In a way it is a summary of my CBS "Basic Theology" course. It is not exclusively related to the salvation theme, but I needed something about this length to fill up the space requirement. (Don't tell anyone!)

Let me remind you that the materials included here in this volume (and in all the others) are mostly incidental writings, and are very focused on specific issues. Thus what you have here is not intended to be a comprehensive explanation of the whole doctrine of salvation. If you want the full, systematic outline of the doctrines of salvation, consult my larger books mentioned earlier.

As usual, Scripture quotations herein are usually from the NASB or ESV, unless noted otherwise.

JACK COTTRELL
September 16, 2018

PART ONE

THREE SERMONS ON SALVATION

THE WELLS OF SALVATION

1 You will say in that day: "I will give thanks to you, O Lord, for though you were angry with me, your anger turned away, that you might comfort me.

2 "Behold, God is my salvation; I will trust, and will not be afraid; for the Lord God is my strength and my song, and he has become my salvation."

3 With joy you will draw water from the wells of salvation. 4 And you will say in that day: "Give thanks to the Lord, call upon his name, make known his deeds among the peoples, proclaim that his name is exalted.

— Isaiah 12:1-4 (ESV)

I grew up in a small country house without indoor plumbing. I remember when we got our drinking water from a well just outside the back door. You had to tie a rope to the water bucket handle, then lower it to the surface of the water. Then you had to give the rope a little flip, so that the bucket would turn over sideways and allow some water to get into it, enough to cause it to sink into the water. Then you pulled the full bucket back out of the well and took it into the kitchen, where there was a dipper that everyone could drink out of. Water for all other purposes was drawn from the well in the same way.

In Bible lands in Bible times, any well was precious, especially one with fresh water fed by an underground spring. (Our well was not; it was just a big deep hole in the ground.) This is illustrated in Genesis 26:12-25, where Isaac and his servants had serious conflicts over wells with the neighboring herdsmen of Philistia and Gerar. The high value placed on wells explains why the Bible would compare the source of our salvation with a well, and the salvation itself with the water from that well. In fact,

Isaiah 12:3 speaks of the wells (plural) of salvation, from which we draw this saving water.

The message here is that God has dug these wells of salvation, and He has invited us to come and draw water from them. What are these wells, and what is the water that comes from them? When you dip your bucket of faith into these wells, what kind of water do you get? Let me suggest that there are three kinds of water that you get from these wells of salvation.

I.   YOU GET WATER TO PUT OUT THE FIRE

The first and most important kind of water that comes from these wells of salvation is water to put out the fire. This is definitely one of the most valuable uses of water. Fire departments know this; their main equipment includes pumper trucks and tanker trucks. I knew this quite early in life. As a child I was guilty of playing with matches one day in a bedroom at one end of our house. A dressing table in that room had a fancy cloth "skirt" around it. My scientific curiosity made me wonder, "Will that burn?" So as a scientific experiment, I held a lit match up to it. Guess what? It burned! Whoops!

I began to walk as fast as possible through the house to the kitchen, which was on the other end of the house. I had to walk through the living room where my Mom was sitting. I hurried to the kitchen, got a dipper of water from the water bucket, and walked really fast back to the fire. I put the water on the fire, but it wasn't enough. Back to the kitchen for another dipper of water. As I was walking fast back through the living room with my dipper full of water again, my Mom stopped me and asked, "What are you doing anyway?" I answered as nonchalantly as I could, "Oh, nothing. Just putting out the fire." She let out a yell and ran to the kitchen and grabbed the whole bucket of water! Fortunately that was enough to put out the fire.

My question here is this: do we as sinners have any fire that needs to be put out? The answer is YES! We are indeed sinners! We have broken

God's laws, and we stand guilty before Him and condemned to eternal punishment in hell. Hell is described as "the lake of fire," "the lake that burns with fire and brimstone, which is the second death" (Revelation 20:15; 21:8). We may argue as to whether this is a literal fire, but that is how the Bible describes it. We need something that will quench the fires of hell for us!

This is exactly what Jesus did for us in His suffering and death on the cross! In His atoning sacrifice He suffered the penalty that we deserve for our sins; He suffered the equivalent of eternity in the lake of fire for us. His blood is that "water" which quenches the fires of hell for us.

This is the first well of salvation: the blood of Jesus Christ. When we dip our faith-bucket into that well as we are going down into the waters of baptism, when we are coming up out of those waters, we are holding a bucketful of forgiveness! This is the same as what the Bible calls "justification." To be justified is to be forgiven, and this is the first and most important thing we get from the wells of salvation. See these Biblical teachings about justification:

- **Romans 3:24-25** – "Being justified as a gift by His grace through the redemption which is in Christ Jesus; whom God displayed publicly as a propitiation" through faith in His blood.
- **Romans 3:28** – "For we maintain that a man is justified by faith apart from" works of law.
- **Romans 4:5** – God is the one who "justifies the ungodly."
- **Romans 5:1** – "Therefore, having been justified by faith, we have peace with God through our Lord Jesus Christ."
- **Romans 5:9** – We are "justified by His blood."

What does it mean to be "justified"? The Greek word is a term that has a legal connotation. It has to do with something that happens in a courtroom, where a defendant is standing before the judge. It refers to what the judge says regarding the fate of the defendant before him. The judge can condemn him and sentence him to pay a penalty; or the judge can JUSTIFY him by pronouncing these words: "NO PENALTY FOR YOU."

A judge usually says this when he finds the defendant to be innocent. But in the heavenly court, there are no innocent defendants. We are all guilty. So how is it possible that the God the Judge can justify us, and say, "No penalty for you"? Because Jesus has already paid that penalty for us! That's what He was doing on the cross! He put out the fires of hell with His own blood, as far as the Christian is concerned. So the Judge is saying, in effect: "I find you guilty as charged. But: no penalty for you."

This is the point of Romans 8:1, which says, "Therefore there is now no condemnation—no penalty, no punishment, no hell—for those who are in Christ Jesus." See how Isaiah 12 expresses this same truth when the prophet is speaking of the wells of salvation: "You will say in that day: 'I will give thanks to you, O Lord, for though you were angry with me, your anger turned away, that you might comfort me. Behold, God is my salvation; I will trust, and will not be afraid'" (vv. 1, 2a).

Think about it: you are a Christian. You sincerely believe in Jesus. There is no hell waiting for you! The fire is out, as far as you are concerned.

I know that many Christians worry about this because they know that they still sin, and are falling short of the glory of God (Romans 3:23). We all know that we are not perfect—and God knows it, too! But here's the thing: under grace, being perfect is not the condition for salvation; trusting in Jesus is! There is no condemnation for those who are in Jesus, and you are in Jesus if you are trusting in Him. In Jesus Christ, you are 100% justified or forgiven.

You are thinking, "But I'm not good enough to go to heaven." Seriously, do you think you can put out the fires of hell by how good you are? Do you think you can douse the lake of fire with your puny good works? That's like me when I was trying to put out that little bedroom blaze with a dipper or two of water, when Mom knew it would take the whole bucket of water! Folks, it takes the blood of Jesus to douse the fires of hell; we are covered by His blood through our faith in Him.

"Not the labors of my hands can fulfill Thy law's demands.
Could my tears forever flow; could my zeal no respite know—
All for sin could not atone. Thou must save, and Thou alone."

No wonder, with JOY we draw water from the wells of salvation!

II. YOU GET WATER THAT GIVES LIFE

The first well of salvation into which we dip our faith-bucket is the well of justification. So is there something more? Yes indeed; there is a second well of salvation; we can call it the well of regeneration. When we draw water from that well, we get the water that gives us life,

This is another main purpose for water. If there is no water, there can be no life. Water is essential for life as we know it. Science fiction writers sometimes create stories about how there may be aliens who have a kind of life that does not need water. I remember a Star Trek episode (I think it was) about silicon-based life forms that looked just like rocks. I saw a cartoon once of an alien humanoid creature whose spaceship had crashed near a big lake here on earth. The creature was dying of thirst, lying next to the lake, and moaning, "Ammonia! Ammonia!"

But we know that life needs water. Our own space probes are desperately searching for traces of water on other orbs in our solar system, trying to prove that there may be life elsewhere in the universe. Anyone who has a garden or even a lawn knows that life needs water. If you have potted plants in your home or office, what happens if you forget to water them? They die! They can be almost dead, but water can revive them.

I know this from another childhood experience, this one a bit more positive than the other one. I saw an ad in a comic book once (yes, I read comic books—they only cost ten cents back then) about a "magic" plant. Order it (for about 25 cents), and it comes to you completely dead. But you put it in a bowl of water, and it gradually turns green and comes back to life! Oh, the power of water! I ordered it, and behold, it really happened.

(This novelty is still advertised in some magazines; they call it the resurrection plant. You should google it; it's quite interesting.)

The question here is, do we sinners have any need for such life-giving water? The answer is YES, absolutely, because unsaved sinners are spiritually dead, dead in their transgressions and sins, as Ephesians 2:1, 5 and Colossians 2:13 specifically say. This means that the sinner's soul is dead toward God, because it is "excluded from the life of God" (Ephesians 4:18). The sinful soul is dead and lifeless with the disease of sin, shriveled, dry, rotten, moldy, decayed in the spiritual and moral sense. Yes, the sinner needs some water that can bring him back to life, that can raise him from the dead.

This is why God has given us the second well of salvation, the well of regeneration, which contains the water of life, the living water that is the Holy Spirit Himself! When Jesus was talking with the Samaritan woman at the well in John 4, He offered to give her "living water." He said, "Whoever drinks of the water that I will give him shall never thirst; but the water that I will give him will become in him a well of water springing up to eternal life" (John 4:14). Later, on a Jewish feast day, Jesus referred to this living water again. In the midst of a water ceremony on that day, "Jesus stood and cried out, saying, 'If anyone is thirsty, let him come to Me and drink. He who believes in Me, as the Scripture said, "From his innermost being will flow rivers of living water"'" (John 7:37-38). On neither of these occasions did Jesus explain that He was referring to the Holy Spirit, but John 7:39 explains it: "But this He spoke of the Spirit, whom those who believed in Him were to receive; for the Spirit was not yet given, because Jesus was not yet glorified" (i.e., ascended into heaven).

This living, saving water from the well of regeneration is accessed when the sinner meets Jesus in Christian baptism. This happens because the Bible says that in that act of baptism, the sinner receives the gift of the Holy Spirit to dwell in "his innermost being" like a river of living water. See Acts 2:38, where Peter gives an invitation to seeking sinners thus: "Repent, and each of you be baptized in the name of Jesus Christ for the forgiveness of your sins, and you will receive the gift of the Holy Spirit." When you dip your faith-bucket into the well of regeneration, Jesus fills it with this living water. From that point on the Holy Spirit dwells within our very souls and bodies (Romans 8:9-10; 1 Corinthians 6:19).

The fact is, like the resurrection plant, we Christians have experienced a real resurrection from the dead. When the Holy Spirit touches our souls in baptism, it is like that "dead" plant coming into contact with water. The essence of life flows back into us. This is how it has happened for you Christians. Ever since your baptism, you have been a new person with new spiritual life. You have received "the washing of regeneration and renewing by the Holy Spirit" (Titus 3:5).

We should be aware, though, that this newness is not felt and experienced all at once. My little "magic" resurrection plant took a couple of days to soak up water and only gradually turned green. This is also the way it happens when we take medicine or have an operation to cure an illness; such treatments do not produce an immediate 100% recovery. The change that happens in baptism is the same. There the process begins, and it takes a lifetime to increase and to come closer and closer to wholeness. So don't give up! Be patient, and work on it. The new life is there; it just needs to be nourished with spiritual food and exercise (see Acts 2:42).

The first moment when you drank from that bucket of living water from the well of regeneration, you were like a butterfly coming out of its cocoon. You may have watched that happen, and you remember that it takes an hour or two for the wings to unfold and dry. But it IS a butterfly; it is no longer a caterpillar. So it is with us who have drunk the living water: we have been changed. You are no longer the old dead sinner you once were. You are a born-again Christian, walking in newness of life (John 3:5; Romans 6:4). You have been raised from death to life (John 5:24).

No wonder, with JOY we draw water from the wells of salvation!

III. YOU GET WATER THAT GIVES
YOU POWER

So far we have seen that the wells of salvation include the well of justification and the well of regeneration. Now we are ready to look at the last one, the well of sanctification. The water from the well of justification puts out the fires of hell for you; the water from the well of regeneration gives you new life. So what do the waters from the well of sanctification do for us? They give us POWER.

This is another vital use and benefit of water: it can be a source of power. For centuries people have used flowing water to turn millstones for the purpose of grinding grain. Men have built great dams across canyons and rivers, to trap water that can be released so as to flow through turbines, thus producing electrical power. The same can be accomplished by boiling water until it becomes steam. Water produces power in many ways.

What about us, and our spiritual lives? Do we have any need for power? Yes! As sinners we were weak and dead in our sins, unable to conform ourselves to God's laws (Romans 8:7-8). Even though we were spiritually dead, we were still able to obey the gospel, which we did. As Christians now, we can say that we are ready to go to work and put our minds to obeying God's law commandments. We are now able to do so, and we are commanded to do so. One problem, though, as explained in the last point, is that we have not yet fully recovered from our old sin-diseased state. Thus we need help in our efforts to be good and do good, and thus to live the Christian life. We need some spiritual power.

Well, that's why there is this third well of salvation, the well of sanctification. This well actually contains the same water as found in the second well, namely, the Holy Spirit. But when drawn from the third well, the living water which is the Holy Spirit affects us as Christians in a slightly different way. Once the Holy Spirit has been given to us in Christian baptism and in that moment has regenerated us, from that time onward He continues to live within our bodies as an indwelling, abiding presence.

Why does the Spirit of God continue to be present within us? Mainly, to give us power. As Isaiah 12:2b says, "For the Lord God is my strength and my song, and he has become my salvation." The Lord God is my strength! This applies especially to God the Holy Spirit. He gives us strength and power. We are not talking here about miraculous power, but about moral power—the power to be good, the power to be holy as God is holy, which we are commanded and expected to be (1 Peter 1:15-16).

When we open ourselves up to the Spirit's presence within us, He strengthens our will to determine to obey God's will in the face of temptations. This is what it means to be "led by the Spirit" (see Romans 8:13-15). The Spirit is not within us to give us knowledge, or to give us mystical guidance, or to help us to know what to do. He has already told us this in the Bible. He is within us to give us the power to do what we already know we should do. That is why Paul prays in Ephesians 3:16, that God would grant you to "be strengthened with power through His Spirit in the inner man." He says in Romans 8:13 that by the Spirit we can put to death the sinful deeds of the body. This is how "God is at work in you," strengthening your will and helping you to obey (Philippians 2:13).

This is the third well of salvation: the Holy Spirit's power to make us holy. Do you want to be a better, holier person? Pray Paul's prayer in Ephesians 3:16 for yourself. Don't try to be good all on your own. This is the very reason God gave you the Holy Spirit in the first place. Pray that you will be open to that power. The main reason why the church often dawdles and flounders around today is that we are not using the Holy Spirit's power for holiness. (Holiness is just another word for sanctification.)

One more illustration from my childhood: the ad I saw for the "resurrection plant" mentioned above may have been in a superhero comic book. The ones I read were Batman, Superman, Plastic Man (my favorite!), and Captain Marvel. I loved the Captain Marvel premise: Billy Batson, a boy not much older than I was, could just say a magic word—Shazam!—and immediately turn into Captain Marvel. I confess that one day I went out to our barn and stood behind it and firmly enunciated that magic word, Shazam, many times. Nothing happened. But my thought was this: what if I am another Billy Batson, and lived all my life without knowing it? What a waste that would be!

That made me think about Clark Kent. What if Clark Kent had lived all his life without knowing he was Superman? What a waste! I can picture him on his deathbed, looking down and saying, "What's that big 'S' on my tee-shirt? Superman? What's that?" How sad.

But folks, there are a lot of Christians who could, in effect, on their deathbeds look down and say, "What's that big 'HS' on my tee-shirt? Holy Spirit? What's that?" This would be even sadder! We already have the source of all the power we need to be the Christians that God wants us to be. Are we using it? Let's do it!

No wonder, with JOY we draw water from the wells of salvation!

CONCLUSION

These are the wells of salvation: 1) The well of justification, from which we draw water that puts out the fires of hell for us; 2) The well of regeneration, from which we draw water that gives us new spiritual life; and 3) The well of sanctification, from which we draw water that gives us the power to live the holy lives that God wants us to live.

Christians—never leave these wells. Stay camped by them and keep drawing from them continually. Keep your faith-bucket full of these waters.

If you are not a Christian, you need to turn to God and obey the gospel, and begin drawing water from these wells of salvation. God invites you to do so. God wants to give you this saving water. Here is His invitation: "Ho! Every one who thirsts, come to the waters; and you who have no money come, buy and eat. Come, buy wine and milk without money and without cost" (Isaiah 55:1). Also, "The Spirit and the bride say, 'Come.' And let the one who hears say, 'Come.' And let the one who is

thirsty come; let the one who wishes take the water of life without cost"
(Revelation 22:17).

"Give thanks to the Lord,
call upon his name,
make known his deeds among the peoples,
proclaim that his name is exalted."

— Isaiah 12:4

THE ROCK OF SALVATION

[14] Therefore, hear the word of the LORD, O scoffers,
Who rule this people who are in Jerusalem,
[15] Because you have said, "We have made a covenant with death,
And with Sheol we have made a pact.
The overwhelming scourge will not reach us when it passes by,
For we have made falsehood our refuge and we have concealed ourselves with deception."
[16] Therefore thus says the Lord GOD,
"Behold, I am laying in Zion a stone, a tested stone,
A costly cornerstone for the foundation, firmly placed.
He who believes in it will not be disturbed.
[17] "I will make justice the measuring line
And righteousness the level;
Then hail will sweep away the refuge of lies
And the waters will overflow the secret place.
[18] "Your covenant with death will be canceled,
And your pact with Sheol will not stand;
When the overwhelming scourge passes through,
Then you become its trampling place.
[19] "As often as it passes through, it will seize you;
For morning after morning it will pass through, anytime during the day or night,
And it will be sheer terror to understand what it means."
— Isaiah 28:14-19

I have written several times on the subject of death, and most of these times one basic theme seems to be emphasized: the idea of human death as an enemy of mankind. In my book, *The Faith Once for All* (College Press, 2002), in the chapter on death, I have a section on "The Character of Death" (pp. 209-214). I begin this section with these words:

In view of the above [Biblical] data it is difficult to view death in anything but a negative way. But for reasons that will be explained below, the fact is that many want to portray death in a most positive light. This temptation must be resisted, and death must be unmasked for what it truly is: the enemy of mankind.... It is the enemy of God, the enemy of Christ, and the enemy of mankind. (p. 209)

Then I describe death as a *reigning* enemy (Romans 5:14, 17), a *feared* enemy (Hebrews 2:14-15), a *deceiving* enemy (Isaiah 28:15), and most of all a *defeated* enemy (Revelation 1:17-18).

Several decades ago I had an article on death published in the *Christian Standard* (8/8/1971) called "In the Face of Death." I pointed out how many if not most people face death with sorrow and dread, and how Jesus faced it with rage (based on the proper translation of the Greek word *embrimaomai* in John 11:33, 38). A reader took issue with me and wrote a letter to the editor (10/31/71), complaining that I was much too negative about death. We should remember, he said, that death is the door to heaven: "Through what other door do I expect to finally see my Lord?" It is death "that gives us entrance to ... the actual presence of God in the fullest of all senses." Also, it is "a welcome rest from suffering. An enemy? Not really."

What the letter writer did not understand (and I apologize for not making it more clear) is that the only reason we can look at death in such positive ways is because, as a true enemy, Jesus Christ has taken it on and defeated it. In this case the defeated enemy does not become our friend; it is still an enemy, though defeated. And what is just as important is that these "positive" aspects of death (which I acknowledge) apply only to Christians. For the mass of mankind that is on the broad way that leads to destruction (Matthew 7:13), death is nothing but their enemy and will be for eternity unless they turn to the only refuge from that enemy, Jesus Christ.

This study, which was a sermon that I have preached many times, is about how Jesus is the only way to avoid the eternal consequences of death.

I. THE RAGING WATERS OF DEATH

A. 1889 – Johnstown, Pennsylvania

In 1889, Johnstown was a small town of about 10,000 people in western Pennsylvania. It was located in a narrow valley with steep sides. About fifteen miles up the valley an earthen dam had been constructed to make a recreational lake for rich people from Pittsburgh. They called it Lake Conemaugh. It was about 450 acres in size, holding about twenty million tons of water (i.e., 4.8 billion gallons).

The people in Johnstown and through the course of the valley were always a bit nervous about the dam, especially when it rained. During Memorial Day week in 1889 it rained *a lot*—long and exceptionally heavy. Sure enough, at 3:10 p.m. on May 31, the dam broke.

When the dam gave way, a witness said the lake behind it just seemed to LEAP into the valley like a living thing, roaring like a mighty battle. The water began moving down the valley—sometimes 70 feet high—at about 40 miles an hour.

The flood advanced as a tremendous wall, pushing ahead of it giant chunks of the dam, fence posts, logs, boulders, whole trees. From below, it looked like a mountain moving. It soon picked up a few small bridges, many mangled houses, dead animals, and indescribable rubbish. It swept through a small town with a railway yard. Now the tidal wave was pushing ahead of it several hundred freight cars, a dozen locomotives, about a hundred more houses, and many human corpses. Just before reaching Johnstown it passed over a large wire factory. Here it picked up a huge cloud of black smoke, plus miles and miles of barbed wire wrapped in rolls.

The people in Johnstown were mostly taken by surprise. Those on the north side of town, toward the dam, heard the noise first. It was like a gigantic wind preceding the raging wall of death. When it came into view, the people saw bearing down on them this huge mass of boxcars, locomotives, houses, hideous masses of barbed wire, plus countless dead cows, horses and human beings.

It was as if the gates of death had suddenly opened, and the enemy was pouring forth with overwhelming force. Over 2,200 people were killed.

B.   2018 – Everywhere, including your home town

To me, this Johnstown flood is a perfect analogy of the way DEATH as such has been relentlessly bearing down upon every one of us from the time we were born. In a sense, we all live in Johnstown, and we all live our lives in the valley of death.

Even in our younger years, we know that death is up that valley, like Lake Conemaugh behind a dam. But we do not see it as an immediate threat, and we do not think too much about it. But as we get older, the rains of life seem to get heavier and heavier. Thus we get more and more nervous about the dam bursting.

Folks, I have news for you: the dam has *already* burst! The raging waters of death are already roaring down that valley!

Most of us already know this. Once we do realize it, we find ourselves staring with horror into that future that is coming hard and swiftly to meet us. We see that future sweeping toward us like the rushing waters of the Johnstown flood. And just as that awful flood thrust ahead of it houses and locomotives and barbed wire and corpses, so we see the future raging toward us with all the debris of death ready to engulf us.

What do we see in that wall of death? Heart disease. Strokes. Leukemia. Lung cancer. Lymphoma. Poisons. Automobile accidents. Kidney failure. Diabetes. Melanoma. Guns and knives in murderers' hands. Malaria. Starvation. HIV. Parkinson's disease. Alzheimer's disease. Pneumonia. Liver cancer. Knee and hip replacements. Lyme disease. We could go on and on.

What can we do to prepare for this inevitable onslaught of the armies of death? How can we come to terms with it?

II. FALSE COVENANTS WITH DEATH

A. 710 B.C. – Jerusalem

How can we prepare for the coming of death? We could put the question another way: how should we NOT prepare for it? The 28th chapter of Isaiah gives us a good example of this. The problem of death was being faced by the city of Jerusalem about 2600 years before the Johnstown flood, in the days of Isaiah the prophet. Here the people of God were facing a specific death threat: the "overwhelming scourge" of the Assyrian armies. Isaiah 28:2 describes them: "Behold, the Lord has a strong and mighty agent; as a storm of hail, a tempest of destruction, like a storm of mighty overflowing waters, He has cast it down to the earth with His hand."

In the eighth century B.C. this overwhelming scourge of Assyrian armies was on the warpath! They were being used by God to punish the ten northern tribes of Israel. In about 722 B.C. the capital city of Samaria was overthrown. And now under King Hezekiah, the southern tribes of God's people are being threatened by Sennacherib, king of Assyria; and Jerusalem is in danger of being swept away by these same overflowing waters. What can they do? These enemies are poised to invade their land, and to destroy the city of Jerusalem and its precious temple. Is there any hope?

"Aha!" said the leaders of the Jews in Jerusalem. "We know! We will escape the danger of death by making a covenant with death itself!" This is what Isaiah is talking about when he refers to their false covenant with death in Isaiah 28:14-15: "Therefore, hear the word of the LORD, O scoffers, who rule this people who are in Jerusalem, because you have said, 'We have made a covenant with death, and with Sheol we have made a pact. The overwhelming scourge will not reach us when it passes by, for we have made falsehood our refuge and we have concealed ourselves with deception.'"

So what did the leaders in Jerusalem decide to do, to ward off the Assyrian enemy? They sought to make a defense treaty with another pagan nation: Egypt! This was their covenant with death itself, their way of protecting themselves from death. "We'll be OK! The Egyptians will protect us!"

This aroused the wrath of God! "You are seeking refuge in lies and falsehoods and deception!" He said. He gave them this warning in Isaiah 30:1-2 and 31:1: "'Woe to the rebellious children,' declares the LORD, 'who execute a plan, but not Mine, and make an alliance, but not of My Spirit, in order to add sin to sin; who proceed down to Egypt without consulting Me, to take refuge in the safety of Pharaoh and to seek shelter in the shadow of Egypt!… Woe to those who go down to Egypt for help … but they do not look to the Holy One of Israel, nor seek the LORD!'"

B.   1889 – Johnstown, Pennsylvania

The residents of Johnstown were like Jerusalem of old; they comforted themselves with false confidence. They joked about the dam up the valley, and told themselves it was fine. "Well, sometime that dam will give way, but it won't happen to us!" When told that the dam was ready to break, many said, "Oh, we've heard that before!" Most thought that if it broke, the level of the river would rise just a few feet.

C.   2018 – Everywhere, including your home town

Nothing seems to change! The floods of death still bear down upon us, and people still trust in Satanic lies and empty covenants with death, hiding behind falsehoods. Some people trust in the hope of reincarnation. Some turn to the occult practice of spiritism, whose motto is "There is no death!" In 1970 Richard Bach published a book called *Jonathan Livingston Seagull*. In 1972 and 1973, it topped the *Publishers Weekly* list of bestselling novels in the United States. It was preaching the "gospel" of spiritism, and people were eating it up. Many are trusting in almighty science to protect them against the enemy death, hoping that research can find a way to stop the aging process, or perfecting cryogenics as a way of someday bringing the body back to life after it has died. Even within the broad boundaries of Christendom, false covenants with death rear their heads in false doctrines such as universal salvation and the denial of hell.

Such attempts to come to terms with death are like the folks at Johnstown in 1889 curling up in a cardboard box in the middle of town and saying, "I'll be OK! No worries!"

What is God's reply to these deceptions? The warnings He gave to Jerusalem still echo down to us in Isaiah 28:17-19:

> I will make justice the measuring line and righteousness the level; then hail will sweep away the refuge of lies and the waters will overflow the secret place. Your covenant with death will be cancelled, and your pact with Sheol will not stand; when the overwhelming scourge passes through, then you will become its trampling place. As often as it passes through, it will seize you; for morning after morning it will pass through, anytime during the day or night, and it will be sheer terror to understand what it means.

So what *is* the solution to this overwhelming scourge, these overflowing waters of death? What does God say?

III. THE ONLY REFUGE FROM DEATH IS THE *ROCK OF SALVATION*, THE RISEN CHRIST

A. God's promise: A STONE TO STAND ON

God gave Israel hope against the Assyrian invasion if they would only accept it. He told them about an unshakable *Rock* that they could stand on for protection. This promise is given in Isaiah 28:16 (Cottrell version): "Therefore thus says the Lord God, 'Behold, I am laying in Zion a stone, a tested stone, a costly cornerstone for the foundation, firmly placed. He who believes in that STONE will never have to run for cover *anywhere else*.'"

Any promise of God is a firm stone upon which we can take a stand, but this one is very special. The Israelites themselves would not understand all that is meant by this stone, but they knew that God was promising to protect them if only they would turn to Him. Today, we know exactly what this promise means. It is a blessed prophecy of the coming Messiah, who would conquer death in all its forms.

B.   God's Son: A ROCK TO REST ON

This prophetic promise of God, in Isaiah 28:16, is the background upon which Jesus makes His grand declaration in Matthew 16:18. This was preceded by this exchange between Jesus and His disciples in vv. 15-17: "He said to them, 'But who do you say that I am?' Simon Peter answered, 'You are the Christ, the Son of the living God.' And Jesus said to him, 'Blessed are you, Simon Barjona, because flesh and blood did not reveal this to you, but My Father who is in heaven.'" Then Jesus shows us what Isaiah's "tested stone" and "costly cornerstone" is referring to: "I also say to you that you are Peter, and upon **this rock** I will build My church; and the gates of Hades will not overpower it."

In Jesus's statement, the ROCK on which the church is built is not the Apostle Peter. The Greek spelling of his name is *petros*, and that is the word Jesus used when He said, "You are *Petros*." But then when He said, "Upon this rock," He used a different but similar word, *petra*. The word for Peter's name, *petros*, means a loose or movable stone; but the word for the church's foundation, *petra*, means solid and immovable rock such as the face of a cliff or bedrock.

What is the identity of this *petra*, this solid Rock on which Jesus would build His church? It is *Himself*, as described in Peter's confession in verse 16. "You are the Christ." This refers to God's anointed one, appointed and anointed to perform the works of redemption. "You are the Son of the living God." This refers to Jesus's divine nature, which is how the title "Son of God" was understood by the Jews in Peter's day. What Jesus says about the contents of this confession in v. 17—that God the Father had revealed it to Peter—shows that this confession is the point of focus in Jesus's reply to Peter. The point is this: Jesus's person (Son of God) and work (the Christ) are the Rock-foundation upon which the church rests.

This reference to Jesus as the Rock-foundation ties this to the Isaiah 28:16 promise. In Isaiah the stone is something to build on as the foundation's cornerstone. Also, Isaiah refers to *believing* in that stone, and the content of Peter's confession is the core of Christian faith, according to John 20:31—"These have been written so that you may believe that Jesus is the Christ, the Son of God." Those who rest their faith upon this Rock need no other protection from our enemies; we will never have to run for cover anywhere else.

And what is the specific enemy Jesus has in mind when He refers to this protective Rock-foundation in Matthew 16:18? He specifies it in the statement, "The gates of Hades will not overpower it." This also clearly ties this text to the one in Isaiah. In Isaiah's prophecy, Sheol is mentioned twice as the enemy with which the Jews had made a pact, in verses 15 and 18. Sheol is the Old Testament equivalent to Hades. This adds to the evidence that Matthew 16:18 is the New Testament version of Isaiah 28:16. And exactly what is this Sheol/Hades? It is the place of *death*, that which represents death in all of its power and destruction. (It is very important NOT to translate Matthew 16:18 as speaking of the "gates of hell." There is no reference here at all to hell.)

But what are the *gates* of Hades? In my judgment Jesus is not referring to a gate leading INTO Hades, but to something like the watergates on a dam which can be opened to let the water pour OUT. Thus the gates of Hades would be the source of the "overwhelming scourge" of death to which Isaiah is referring. The point is that Jesus is the only refuge that can protect us from the forces of death or the powers of death (as some versions translate it). This applies only to those who *believe* in that Stone.

C. God's Church: A HOUSE TO HIDE IN

There is one further aspect to Jesus's work of rescuing us and hiding us from the enemy, death. If Jesus is the *foundation*, that means something will be built upon Him. And His declaration tells us what that is: the church. Jesus the Rock-foundation says He will build upon this foundation an indestructible shelter from the flood of death. This shelter is the church.

(Jesus here uses future tense, because He did not begin to build the church until the Day of Pentecost in Acts 2.)

When the floodwaters of Lake Conemaugh rampaged through Johnstown, *one* building that withstood the onslaught was a massive stone Methodist Church. It held, split the wave, and shielded several buildings behind it and those sheltered there. One person was heard to shout afterwards, "We've been saved by the Methodist Church!"

I don't know about the *Methodist* church, but I do know that *JESUS'S* church saves us from the universal flood of death. The church which is our sure shelter is not some stone building, but the spiritual body of believers who trust in Jesus.

Why is Christ's church the answer to death? Not because there is saving power in the church itself, but because of the *solid Rock* on which it is built—the ROCK OF REFUGE, THE STONE OF SAFETY, JESUS HIMSELF. *Jesus* is the stone laid for this very purpose. The stone specifically is Jesus in his saving work, His death on the cross and His resurrection from the grave. In His death Jesus stood in the path of the flood of death, and let it sweep over Him—locomotives, barbed wire, cancer, Alzheimer's, leukemia, and all. He absorbed the full *penalty* and *power* of death (see Hebrews 2:14). But three days later, after this flood passed, we look—and Jesus is *still standing!* The risen Christ has conquered death! And He is *our* stone of shelter and safety from its terrifying flood.

The resurrection of Jesus from the dead is our guarantee that death will not destroy or defeat us. Because of Jesus the ROCK, we are prepared for that death-dam to break. Yes, we hear the roar of that flood of death as it comes bearing down on us. Yes, we see the devasting debris of death as it rushes toward us from the future. We are in its path; we cannot escape it. *But we do not fear it,* because we are trusting in Jesus, the risen Christ. We are standing on the ROCK, and taking shelter behind Him and in His church.

As Christians, we are ready for it. Let it come! Let our last breath leave the body, and let this body be covered in a grave! We will still win! Our *spirits* will immediately go to be with the risen Jesus, and in the last day the risen Jesus will also give us *new bodies* like His own. We win! We beat the flood of death! So – even though we walk through the valley of the shadow of death, we will fear no evil, because the risen Jesus, our strong sheltering Rock, is with us. As Ira Sankey wrote it,

The Lord's our Rock, in Him we hide—a shelter in the time of storm.
Secure whatever ill betide—a shelter in the time of storm.

The raging storms may 'round us beat—a shelter in the time of storm.
We'll never leave our safe retreat—a shelter in the time of storm.

O Rock divine, O Refuge dear—a shelter in the time of storm.
Be thou our helper ever near—a shelter in the time of storm.

Oh, Jesus is a Rock in a weary land—a weary land, a weary land.
Oh, Jesus is a Rock in a weary land—a shelter in the time of storm.

THE ROBE OF RIGHTEOUSNESS

I first began to understand what it means to be saved by grace by being exposed to the teachings of the Protestant Reformers, especially Martin Luther. This first happened while I was a student at Westminster Theological Seminary, 1962-1965; then later at Princeton Seminary, 1967-1969. During that time I was preaching on most Sundays, including a lot of supply and guest preaching during the summers, visiting many different congregations. Early in that period I developed one sermon that I felt represented the essence of grace, which is the one that follows here. And I was also aware that our churches needed to hear and understand the message of grace, so I preached this sermon over and over during those years—close to sixty times.

When I began my teaching career as the associate professor of theology at the Cincinnati Bible Seminary graduate school in the fall of 1967, I was scheduled to preach my first chapel sermon that semester. I decided to preach this sermon. I made that decision with a bit of apprehension, knowing that the Restoration Movement had been rather weak in its grasp of the essence of grace. But I plunged ahead, and preached the version of the sermon that follows here, which is a bit more academic than the usual church version.

At the end of a chapel sermon in those days, it was customary for faculty members to come forward in order to greet and express thanks to the speaker. The first to greet me was my boss, the dean of the graduate school, the eminent Dr. Lewis Foster. He had kind words for me, but also some critical remarks about things I should have added or said in different ways. Gulp! Then I noticed that, coming up behind him, was his father, the honorable and intensely revered Professor R. C. Foster, one of the founders of the school— staring at me rather severely. My apprehension increased. He walked up to me (double gulp!), then smiled and reached out and kindly shook my trembling hand and said (words similar to this—I don't remember for sure): "Wonderful sermon, Brother Cottrell! We are so glad to have you aboard!"

I cannot express how relieved I felt when he said that. Ever since then I have been "full steam ahead" in the proclamation of God's wonderful grace.

This message appeared in print in the *Christian Standard*, February 7 & 14, 1971. It is included here with permission of Christian Standard Media. I have here used the 1995 NASB for Scripture quotations.

INTRODUCTION

The Apostle Paul wanted to preach the gospel to the people of Rome in person, but he was never able to carry out his own plans to go to Rome. He was always hindered, as he says (probably after the pattern of Acts 16:6; God had His own plan for Paul's visit to Rome). So not being able to preach the gospel in person, he did the next best thing: he wrote the gospel to the Romans in a letter (see Romans 1:11-15).

So what do we have in the book of Romans? We have here Paul's own studied statement of the gospel. It is the gospel in its fullest and deepest form. What can it be but the grandest truth which Jesus Christ Himself promised to reveal through the Holy Spirit (John 16:12-15)? It is truth so glorious and so sublime that even our Lord Himself could not reveal it before His death and resurrection, for even the apostles could not have understood it then.

But now, through the Apostle Paul, the Holy Spirit does reveal that which deserves to be called gospel—"good news"—in the fullest sense of the word.

We of the Restoration Movement rejoice in the New Testament church. We rejoice in the privilege to preach and teach the simple and everlasting gospel. But I fear that in both teaching and practice we have yet to restore that which is the very heart of the New Testament: the gospel according to Paul.

We have often limited our definition of the gospel to Paul's statement in 1 Corinthians 15:3-4 concerning the death, burial, and resurrection of Christ. We have limited the gospel to the Gospels, or to the facts of the earthly life of Jesus. Then we have led people to this gospel, in light of the external pattern discernible in the Book of Acts.

But where is the book of Romans? Too often it remains like a book "sealed up with seven seals," while preachers of the gospel avoid it, pleading "I am unworthy to open the book and to loose the seals thereof." How many times have our weekly prayer meetings "gone through" the book of Acts, in comparison with the book of Romans?

To avoid the gospel according to Paul is like laying the foundation of a house and never building the house itself. It is like buying a ticket to the theater and then staying in the lobby. To omit the central message of Romans from the proclamation of the gospel is like buying the marriage license and going through the ceremony, and then never entering into the fullness of married love.

Until we have wrestled with and been conquered and blessed by the book of Romans, we have not yet climbed to the heights of the gospel.

The gospel according to Paul is summed up in Romans 1:16-17, "For I am not ashamed of the gospel, for it is the power of God for salvation to everyone who believes, to the Jew first and also to the Greek. For in it the righteousness of God is revealed from faith to faith; as it is written, 'But the righteous man shall live by faith.'"

It is difficult to imagine that someone could read this passage and be led to hate God because of it. But this was exactly the experience of Martin Luther, when he was still a Roman Catholic monk. How could the gospel, which is supposed to be good news, bring him to such a state? Because he interpreted the "righteousness of God" to be the robe of justice with which God, the righteous judge, clothes Himself and on the basis of which He condemns us guilty sinners to hell. Only gradually did Luther come to see that the righteousness of God revealed in the gospel is like a robe of righteousness which God gives to us guilty sinners in order to cover our own unrighteousness. When Luther finally perceived that this is the gospel according to Paul, the chains of fear with which the Roman Catholic Church had bound him were broken with a mighty hallelujah, the echo of which can still be heard today, though very faintly at times.

What is there about the gospel that gives it such liberating power? It is the fact that in the gospel is revealed a wholly new way of being justified, of being right with God. It is not new in God's plan, and is even foretold, foreshadowed, and applied in Old Testament times. But for sinners who hear and truly understand the gospel for the first time, it is a wholly new way of thinking about salvation compared to how the world understands it. For sinners and even for Christians who for all their lives have been trapped in the darkness of law-righteousness, the gospel has a way of bursting out like a light suddenly being turned on in the midst of that darkness. What is this wholly new and different way of being right with God? It is the way of grace, instead of the way of law. The gospel is the idea that in Christ we approach God not according to law (our obedience and disobedience as measured by God's law), but according to grace (God's willingness freely to forgive our disobedience). We are right with God not through works of law but through faith.

The central theme of the gospel according to Paul is expressed very clearly in the Biblical concept of the *robe of righteousness*. The gospel reveals the fact that God justifies (i.e., forgives) us by giving a robe of righteousness to those who put their trust in Him. Here are three basic facts concerning this robe of righteousness: we need it; we do not have it; God gives it.

I.   WE NEED A ROBE OF RIGHTEOUSNESS.

The first basic fact is that we need a robe of righteousness. Anyone who hopes to dwell in the presence of the holy God for eternity must be clothed in suitable garments. Certain occasions in this life call for appropriate clothing. We do not wear the same clothing when cleaning out the garage as when attending church. A big wedding always demands our very best and fanciest outfit. Likewise, when we appear before God on Judgment Day, and if we hope to dwell with Him forever, we must be properly dressed. (The idea of presentable clothing, of course, is here a figure of speech or an analogy representing what it means to "be right with God.")

What is the proper garment to wear in the presence of God? Can it be anything other than a robe of righteousness? Can we hope to stand (i.e., be sustained) before God in judgment without it? See Psalms 1:5.

The robe of righteousness is not just a matter of proper etiquette; it is an absolute necessity. We need it. Concerning the beautiful heavenly city, the New Jerusalem, Revelation 21:27 says that "nothing unclean, and no one who practices abomination and lying, shall ever come into it." The parable of the wedding feast (Matthew 22:1-13) makes it very clear that if we do not have on the right clothing, we shall be cast away from God's presence forever.

Now, one way to think of God's law is that it is meant to be a pattern that shows us how to sew a robe of righteousness. It shows us how our robe must look. That is to say, it shows us how we must conduct our lives in order to be acceptable to God.

The gospel does not remove this requirement. The gospel does not remove the need for a robe of righteousness. There is no relaxing of the standards. In Romans 1:16-17 righteousness is still inseparably connected with eternal life. So the good news is not that God no longer requires righteousness. If anything, the gospel intensifies the requirements of the ethical and religious life.

Thus, we NEED a robe of righteousness.

II. WE DO NOT HAVE A ROBE OF RIGHTEOUSNESS.

The second basic fact revealed in the book of Romans—the gospel according to Paul—is that we *do not have* a robe of righteousness.

This is terrifyingly impressed upon us by the words of Isaiah 64:6, "For all of us have become like one who is unclean, and all our righteous deeds are like a filthy garment." Or as the KJV puts it, "All our righteousnesses are as filthy rags." We must be very careful not to unconsciously take this passage as a description of our sins. Isaiah does not say that our sins are as filthy rags, but our righteousnesses, our good works!

This means that all our attempts to sew a robe of righteousness for ourselves out of our own good works will fail miserably. No matter how hard we may try, our own efforts and works and righteousnesses are completely incapable of making us acceptable to God. To think otherwise is to make the mistake of the Pharisee in Christ's parable, the one who wore his own righteousness in God's presence and who Jesus said was not justified (see Luke 18:9-14.)

No wonder the Apostle Paul said that when Judgment Day comes, he wants to be found "in Him, not having a righteousness of my own derived from the Law" (Philippians 3:9). Now surely, if anyone could claim salvation on the basis of personal righteousness, it should be Paul. But Paul knew the point of Isaiah 64:6. He knew that even his best personal garment was nothing but filthy rags in God's sight. And if this is true of Paul, how much more is it true of us!

This is why we cannot be justified by a system of law and works of law—any law. This includes not just the Old Testament or the Mosaic law, but any set of commandments and prohibitions which promises reward for obedience and punishment for disobedience. Even the Sermon on the Mount or the book of Romans itself, considered as law codes, will condemn us and not justify us!

In this connection there are two ways in which we can very easily miss the whole point of Romans and thereby obscure the gospel. One of these is by interpreting "law" in Romans as referring to the Old Testament or Mosaic law in every instance. This is very commonly done, but it cannot be defended. In many cases there is no definite article preceding the word "law." More significantly, the main point of Romans 1:18-3:20 is that all men know God's law, have broken God's law, and stand condemned by God's law. This includes both Jews and Gentiles—namely, both those who have access to the Bible and those who do not. Everyone is condemned by whatever form of law applies to him. Also, such basic passages as Romans

3:28 and 6:14 show that it is not a particular law but law as such—legalism—that is being condemned. Paul is saying that we cannot use the system or framework of law as a means of approaching God. The fact of sin makes this impossible.

This first error leads to a second way of obscuring the gospel, namely, by making the New Testament a new law which replaces the Old Testament but is still a law which must be used as a legalistic approach to God. While rejoicing that we are no longer under the old law, we proceed to use the new law in exactly the same way the Jews tried to use the old law—as a pattern by which we must attempt to tailor our own robe of righteousness. We feel that somehow the pattern is clearer and brighter and easier, and therefore we ought to be able now to make that robe of righteousness which the Old Testament saints could not.

This is a fatal delusion which must be abandoned before it is too late. God condemned and rejected the Jews not because they could not live up the requirements of the Old Testament law, but because they were using this law in the wrong way—as a means of establishing their own righteousness before God (Romans 10:3). Likewise we shall be condemned if we try to use New Testament law commandments in the same way; for to all those who believe, Christ is the end of law (no definite article) as a means of establishing one's righteousness (Romans 10:4). Even under the New Testament, our personal righteousness is filthy rags. It is a terrible mistake to think that the New Testament pattern for holiness is simpler and easier to follow than that of the Old Testament. If anything, the Christian revelation profoundly intensifies the requirements for holiness, as meditation on the Sermon on the Mount would show. The New Testament only sharpens the contrast between our rags and the required robe; it makes it clearer than ever that we do not have a robe of righteousness.

So here is the sad truth. We need this robe, but we do not have it. But where is the gospel, the good news? Is everything as hopeless as it sounds? By no means! It is only when we recognize how desperate our situation is that we can appreciate just how good the good news of the gospel is. Only when we have grasped the above two main points are we ready for the gospel.

III. GOD GIVES US THE REQUIRED ROBE OF RIGHTEOUSNESS.

Our third point is the good news (gospel) itself! This good news is that God gives us the very robe of righteousness which He requires. The prophet Isaiah exclaims in Isaiah 61:10, "I will rejoice greatly in the Lord, my soul will exult in my God; for He has clothed me with garments of salvation, He has wrapped me with a robe of righteousness."

This is the way Paul thinks of the righteousness of God in Romans. It is the gift of righteousness which God freely bestows upon those who put their trust in Him instead of in themselves. This righteousness of God is revealed in the gospel (Romans 1:17). It is revealed apart from law (Romans 3:21). Christ has brought an end to trusting in self-righteousness (Romans 10:4).

This righteousness which God gives us is the forgiveness of sins earned by Christ's atoning death on the cross. When we put our trust in Christ's death and are baptized into Him, we "put on Christ" (Galatians 3:27)—and this is when we don the robe of righteousness. We are now "in Christ Jesus," who has been made our righteousness (1 Corinthians 1:30). "He made Him who knew no sin to be sin on our behalf, so that we might become the righteousness of God in Him" (2 Corinthians 5:21). So "put on the Lord Jesus Christ" (Romans 13:14)!

Paul's best statement of this is actually not in Romans but in Philippians 3:9, where he says he wants to "be found in Him, not having a righteousness of my own derived from the Law, but that which is through faith in Christ, the righteousness which comes from God on the basis of faith." A familiar hymn is based on this verse (and Isaiah 61:10):

My hope is built on nothing less than
Jesus's blood and righteousness....

When He shall come with trumpet sound,
oh, may I then in Him be found,
Dressed in His righteousness alone ... .

May we not make the mistake (as I did in my youth) of unconsciously interpreting the first lines of this hymn as "My hope is built on nothing less than Jesus's blood and MY righteousness." There is nothing further from the gospel.

We must see the radical nature of this means of being justified, of being counted righteous before God. The gospel is not just a change in the content of the law. It is a completely different system of justification, a different approach to being righteous. What the gospel reveals is a way of being justified that is new to most sinners: grace, not law. The basic contrast in Romans is not between the Old Testament law and the New Testament law, but rather between *law as such*, and *grace*. The Old Testament law is just one example of law. Thus the contrast is between two wholly different frameworks of thought and action. Grace gives us a new frame of reference and requires a different kind of response on our part: faith, not works of law (Romans 3:28).

The radical difference between law and grace may be stated thus. Under law God supplies the pattern, and we supply all the materials and energy to try to make our own robe of righteousness. Under grace God supplies not only the pattern but the robe itself, which He offers to us as a free gift. What He requires of us is a wholehearted faith or trust in His promises, namely, His promises to give us this robe of righteousness in baptism and to continue to clothe us with it as long as we are surrendered to Him in complete trust.

What does this mean to us? It means that we are made presentable to God not by our works, not by things we do, but by that which Christ has done for us. We cannot think of our deeds as patches with which we are trying to sew some kind of crazy-quilt garment of our own, one which will clothe us adequately before God. Be not deceived! All our righteousnesses are as filthy rags!

Here is the very reason millions of Christians fail to have a sense of assurance of their salvation. Still operating within the framework of law, they feel their salvation depends upon their achieving a certain level of righteousness. But they are frustrated and terrified by the awareness of their own inadequacy and unworthiness and inability to "cut it according to the pattern."

No wonder there is no "blessed assurance" here. Genuine assurance is impossible within the framework of law, where one feels his salvation rests upon his own worthiness and righteousness. Anyone who says he feels secure because he has done enough or because he is good enough is deceiving himself and mocking the grace of God. All these things are sinking sand; Christ alone is the solid Rock! It is the righteousness of His shed blood alone which justifies us; we have no other plea. Let us cease this false trust in ourselves, which can lead only to self-deception or self-despair; and let us humbly accept the robe of righteousness which God gives us.

This is what Christian liberty is all about. The truth that God gives us the required robe of righteousness is the truth that makes us free (see John 8:32). It frees us from frustration, from despair, and from fear of death and judgment. It thereby frees us from self-centeredness and preoccupation with our own salvation. The gospel thus frees us for concentration on truly good works, for service to God and to our neighbor out of pure, unselfish love and not out of hope for personal reward.

Indeed, this is what it means to be free from law. It is not just freedom from the minutiae of Old Testament ordinances. Most significantly, it is freedom from the idea that how well we are doing in personal obedience to His law is the way we will be accepted by God (Romans 10:4). (It is definitely not, however, freedom from law as a binding guide for godly living, as Romans 6 shows. We still have an absolute obligation to *obey*

God's laws, even though our salvation is not determined by how successful we are at fulfilling this obligation.)

No wonder the gospel is dynamite (*dynamis*, Romans 1:16), a dynamite-like power which can move sinners to accept it when it is presented in all its depth! It truly is good news—the best news ever—that God gives us the very robe of righteousness that He requires. The gospel shows us, if we will only see it, that our salvation depends not on our weakness but on God's strength.

> *"When He shall come with trumpet sound,*
>> *oh, may I then in Him be found—dressed*
> *in HIS righteousness alone!"*

PART TWO

ROMANS AND GALATIANS

THE MESSAGE OF ROMANS 1-8: A DEVOTIONAL

INTRODUCTION

How can we discern what Paul is teaching in Romans 1-8, or what any other Biblical text means, for that matter? The issue is not just hermeneutics. Rather, to a great extent it depends on how we answer this question: *who is the primary AUTHOR of the Bible?* This is a watershed issue—in Christendom, in Evangelicalism, in the Restoration Movement, and in many colleges and seminaries. Christian orthodoxy usually agrees that Scripture has TWO authors: the human and the divine. But which is determinative? Which is in control? Which has the final say?

In matters of Biblical interpretation today, a common approach is that the key to discerning the meaning of a text or a book of the Bible is understanding the human context in which that book arose. I.e., the intended meaning of a Biblical text or book is supplied by the human author, in the sense that it must be something already within the experiences or thought processes of that writer. Thus to really know what a text or book means, we have to know the background and circumstances of the writer. Only then can we be sure what the writing is all about.

This is the presupposition of something today called the "New Perspective on Paul" [NPP], as represented by N. T. Wright, for example. This view says that up until about 1961, everyone completely misunderstood Paul's writings. They assumed that Paul's focus is on *personal salvation from sin*, via justification by faith in Christ's substitutionary atonement rather than by good works. In writing about this Paul was opposing legalism or works-salvation, mainly as it was held by the Jews of his day. But the NPP says that this understanding of Paul is completely wrong; it is "foreign to the apostle," as N. T. Wright says. Why did everyone before 1961 go wrong? Because they did not understand the Rabbinic traditions that shaped Paul's ideas; they had no access to, or neglected, the many extrabiblical Jewish writings that Paul was no doubt steeped in.

So how can we interpret Paul aright? At last, some 1900 years after Paul, and after 1900 years of misunderstanding him, someone has *finally* seen the light! Now we know, thanks to the NPP, that to understand Paul we must dig deeply into these extrabiblical Jewish writings from the intertestamental era (called the era of second-temple Judaism, c. 515 B.C. to A.D. 70). When we do this we will realize that the Jews of Paul's day, including Paul himself, "were not sitting around discussing how to go to heaven" (as Wright puts it). Thus for hundreds of years Protestants and Evangelicals have missed the point, e.g., of Romans. But since we now know the human context in which Paul's thought processes developed, we can at last know the mind of Paul, and the real meaning of his writings, especially Romans.

I have been studying and teaching Romans for over 50 years, admittedly with very little knowledge of the Rabbinic literature which the NPP glorifies. But I have had a firm conviction that the main author of Romans is not Paul but the HOLY SPIRIT, and that the Holy Spirit knows about and is addressing issues that are not limited to and restricted by what the Jewish scholars of first century Judaism believed. Paul himself tells us that the things he taught were not received from any man, but were received through a revelation of Jesus Christ (Galatians 1:11-13). Thus I believe that the message of Paul as revealed and inspired by the Holy Spirit is a message that applies to, and can be understood by, not just those familiar with the first-century Jewish context. Rather, it addresses the spiritual needs of all peoples of all ages and cultures. It can be understood by and applied to anyone, in all contexts and circumstances.

I. THE MAIN MESSAGE OF ROMANS 1-8

The key idea in Romans is in 6:14, that "you are not under law but under grace."

To understand this, and to understand Romans, you MUST understand the phrase, "not under law." And to understand this, you MUST understand how Paul is using the word "law." The main point is this: you will completely misunderstand Paul (and Romans) if you erroneously think that every time Paul uses the term "law" (Greek, *nomos*), he means THE LAW OF MOSES.

Sometimes that may be the case, but in his general teaching, when Paul is talking about law as a code of conduct we creatures are obligated to obey, he is referring to ALL such law codes, including the heart-code known even by pagans or Gentiles (Romans 2:14-15), and the law commands addressed to all people in the New Covenant writings.

How do we know "law" has this universal or general application in Romans? We know this, not because we have studied the Rabbinic literature of Paul's time, but because of the way Paul uses the term in his writings. When we examine the texts themselves, we see that what Paul says about "law" (*nomos*) applies to Gentiles in 1:18-32; 2:14-15; and in Romans 4 he uses Abraham as the major example for his main thesis. Neither the Gentiles nor Abraham were under the Mosaic Law.

Thus what Paul writes applies to everyone, including Christians, in reference to the law by which we are supposed to live as revealed in the hundreds of law commands and instructions in the New Testament writings. We do not need to know anything about the Law of Moses and Rabbinic writings to get Paul's point in Romans! Forget about the Law of Moses (well, not literally)! Our "law" includes New Testament texts such as Romans 12-13, and Ephesians 4-5!

So what is the point of Romans 6:14, that "you are not under law but under grace"? Simply this: even though Christians (like everyone else) *are* under a LAW CODE (e.g., Romans 12-13; Ephesians 4-5) as a *way of life*, they are *not* under the LAW SYSTEM, which is the *way of entering heaven* via perfect obedience to your law code (e.g., Romans 12-13; Ephesians 4-5). Romans 6:14 is making a point not about any specific law code, but about the impotence of the *law system* (i.e., law-keeping as the key to eternal life). No one will actually be saved (enter heaven) by the law system, since "all have sinned." Christians are, however, under the GRACE SYSTEM, which is the way of entering heaven via trusting in God's promises to save us by His grace and especially by the saving work of Jesus Christ. That is the point of Romans 1-8.

II. HOW TO EXPLAIN THIS KEY THEME OF ROMANS

Here I have affirmed that the key theme of Romans is that Christians are not under law, but under grace, as expressed in 6:14-15. Now I want to emphasize the point of this affirmation. What issue is it addressing? What does this have to do with our lives? Basically, it is the key to understanding whether we are JUSTIFIED or not, i.e., whether our sins are forgiven, and thus whether we are in a right *relationship* with God and accepted before the law.

As human beings created in God's image, our normal or natural relationship to God is established by means of LAW. This has been so ever since the beginning (see Genesis 1:28; 2:15-17). By virtue of creation, we *should* be "under law," living in full obedience to our law code and accepted by God on that basis. This means that our right relationship to God should be based on *our own righteousness*. We should be *justified by works*.

So what is the problem? The problem is SIN, and therefore a broken relationship with God, leading to our ultimate eternal separation from God. (Every individual repeats the pattern of Genesis 1-3.)

The question, then, is this: Can our relationship with God be restored? This is what Paul is addressing in Romans. The answer is: YES—but not in terms of the original, simple, natural means of *law*. In order to restore our relationship with God, and to maintain it as such, some completely different means of relating to God must be provided.

Here is where Paul begins his message in Romans: if you want to get back into that right relationship with God—a right standing before God our Creator, Lawgiver, and Judge—you cannot do it with your law code! You cannot do it by how well you obey the law's commandments!

For an illustration: in the beginning, humanity's right relationship with the transcendent God was like a great BRIDGE spanning the gulf between Creator and creatures. That bridge is THE LAW. Creatures were given the ability to traverse that bridge via our obedience to our law code; we were accepted by God via our own righteousness—a LAW righteousness. But sin has destroyed the bridge! It has collapsed and lies in ruins, and is impossible to travel across. Thus we are separated from God. Now what? Is it possible that we ourselves might rebuild the bridge, using our own resources? Is it possible that we might work our way across the separating gulf by manipulating the wreckage of the first bridge? Can the law-bridge somehow lead us back to God?

Paul's message in Romans begins with a resounding NO to this question. By works of law—by our own efforts at re-establishing our relationship with God based on our own righteousness—NOBODY will be justified before God—*period*! (This is the point of Romans 1:18 – 3:20.)

BUT—the all-powerful, all-loving, all-wise Creator-God has from the beginning been ready to set into motion a NEW plan, a *substitute* plan, an unnatural yet absolutely foolproof way of re-uniting us with Himself!

This amazingly different, practically unbelievable way of being accepted by God does not depend on *our* ability to find a way to cross the chasm that separates us from God. We do not have the resources or the strength to rebuild the law-bridge, or to devise some other way to get right with God. Even if God Himself were to rebuild and reopen that original bridge, sin has weakened us to the point that we would not be able to make our way across it anyway.

Thus God has provided for us a different way to be in a right relationship with Himself—a way that depends not on what *we* can do (i.e., our own righteousness) but on what *someone else* does. That someone else is Jesus Christ, God the Son incarnate. Jesus has made available to us a different way of crossing the great divide between us and God. Instead of a *bridge of law*, He has prepared for us a BOAT OF GRACE; and He invites us to board that boat and let HIM carry us back into the presence of God with HIS works, HIS power, HIS righteousness. He invites us to *believe* in Him, to believe that He has done and can do what is necessary to bring us back to an eternally happy relationship with God.

This is what Paul is explaining to us in Romans 3:21 – 5:21. He has already said that we cannot be justified by our own righteousness, by our obedience to the law code that applies to us. But God has provided *another way* to be accepted (i.e., justified): the way of grace.

It is important that we understand the *meaning* of justification: God as Judge declares, "No penalty for you!" We must also understand the *basis* for this declaration toward sinners: the death of Jesus as a redemption and as a propitiation. This prepares us to focus on the question of HOW WE CAN ACCESS this justification under the GRACE system. Under law, we would be justified by our own righteousness. But under grace, we are justified by GOD'S righteousness—which is Christ's satisfaction of the law's requirement for *penalty*, a transaction which He freely offers to transfer/impute to us, if we … WHAT?

Here is where we encounter the great doctrine of JUSTIFICATION BY FAITH. This can also be expressed as "justification by grace," justification by Christ's blood (Romans 5:9), and as "justification by God's righteousness." These latter phrases emphasize the actual BASIS of our justification, while the concept of "justification by faith" emphasizes the MEANS by which we access it.

Coming back to the illustration of the grace-boat (which takes the place of the law-bridge), the question is this: how can we get on that boat of grace? Picture the boat being anchored just off-shore, and imagine a loudspeaker on the boat broadcasting instructions on how to board.

The Roman Catholic Church developed its own approach to salvation over the hundreds of years of the Middle Ages. It put much emphasis on the sacraments, especially on penance. A main point of the Protestant Reformation was to challenge this Catholic view of salvation, and to reconstruct a view more in keeping with what Paul is teaching in Romans.

Several different versions of "the way of salvation" (the *ordo salutis*) have been developed within Protestantism, though. One is Calvinism, which says that all sinners are like dead bodies lying on the ground, unable to hear the loudspeaker or to make any move toward boarding the grace-boat. God Himself decides to save *some* of the sinners, and just leave the rest behind. So He picks up the dead bodies of the chosen and carries them aboard the boat, where they miraculously come back to life. These chosen ones have absolutely no part in the choice or the change. Nor is there any danger that they will ever fall off the boat.

Another version is Free-Will Protestantism. Here, all sinners are still spiritually conscious and able to hear the invitation to board the grace-boat. But how? The answer is: simply believe. Then, at the very moment of faith, God immediately forgives and regenerates you and "beams you up" (transports, teleports you) onto the boat. This is the free-will version of the Zwinglian doctrine of "faith alone," or *sola fidei*.

In traditional Restoration Movement thinking, the loudspeaker is instructing sinners to believe the offer of grace, to repent of their sins, to confess faith in Jesus, and to be immersed in water for the forgiveness of their sins. (Regarding the last point, in the boat illustration, the ship is anchored a bit offshore. When the sinner makes his move to enter it, he must go into the water in order to reach it. As he goes down into the water, he steps off the shore of sin; when he comes up out of the water, he is on the grace boat.) Unfortunately, though, according to this traditional thinking, every time the saved person commits a sin, he falls off the boat, and must grab a rescue-rope (a repentant confession of that sin) to be hauled back aboard. He lives in fear that he may perish before he gets around to grabbing the rope. (This is a form of Galatianism.)

In Biblical Restorationism the details are mostly the same, except in the last scene, every time a saved person sins he does not fall off the boat; he does not lose his salvation. Except for the sin of unbelief, a sin is more like falling down while on the boat, and needing help to get up and to get stronger so as not to fall down again. The only way to actually fall off the boat is to stop believing in its Skipper.

III. THE OUTLINE OF ROMANS 1-8.

A. Introduction to Romans as a whole: 1:1-17.

B. The first main point: the impotence of the law system of salvation, 1:18-3:20. NO ONE can be saved by the law system, because this would require perfect obedience to one's law code, and no one has such perfect obedience. ALL HAVE SINNED.

   1. *Gentiles* are all sinners, and thus cannot be saved by their law code, 1:18-32; 2:14-15.

   2. *Jews* are likewise all sinners, and thus cannot be saved via their law code, i.e., the Mosaic Law, 2:1 – 3:8.

   3. *All* are thus sinners, 3:9-20; and as a consequence, "by works of law"—i.e., by how well you keep your law code, whichever one that happens to be—"no flesh will be justified in his sight" (v. 20).

C. The second main point: God has provided the grace system as the only workable alternative to salvation by law-keeping, 3:21 – 8:39. Salvation by grace includes three aspects: The "first work of grace," and the main element of grace, is *justification*, which is the judge's declaration to a defendant: "No penalty for you!" Under grace, "one is justified by faith apart from works of law" (3:28). Justification is a legal concept; it is the same as forgiveness of sins. Forgiveness of sins, 3:21-5:21.

1. The basis for such justification is the propitiatory work of Christ, the substitutionary atonement, 3:24-26.

2. The one MEANS of access to this saving work of Christ is FAITH in Him, APART FROM a consideration of "works of law," i.e., how well we have obeyed our law code (3:28). (There are other conditions for receiving grace in addition to faith, but faith is the sole MEANS for receiving it.)

3. A prime example of this way of salvation is Abraham, chapter 4.

4. The blessed result of knowing you are justified by faith is assurance of salvation, chapter 5. This is affirmed in a general way in 5:1-11, and it is affirmed in a specific way in 5:12-21. The point of the latter passage is not original sin, but original grace. If we believe the whole human race can be subjected to sin and death through one act of one man (i.e., Adam), then we have "much more" (vv. 15, 17) reason to believe that everything brought on us by Adam has been and will be nullified and removed by one act of the one man who is more than a man: Jesus Christ.

D. The "second work of grace" is sanctification, 6:1 – 8:13.

1. Even though we are justified by faith and not by how well we keep our law code, we are still obligated to obey the law code given to us under the New Covenant. The grace system does not liberate us from our absolute creaturely obligation to obey the Creator's commands.

2. But grace is at work here, too, in a way that is different from justification, namely: regeneration (spiritual resurrection) of

our spiritually-dead souls/spirits in baptism, and the resulting sanctification (growth in holiness) through the indwelling Holy Spirit (who provides inward spiritual power for obedience).

3. During our Christian life on this earth, we are "half-saved" (as John Stott says), since the soul/spirit has experienced renewal, though the body is still under the power of sin. See 8:10, NASB.

E. The "third work of grace" is glorification, 8:14 – 39.

1. Our souls/spirits are glorified (perfectly sanctified) when the body dies. This is not mentioned in Romans, but is confirmed by Hebrews 12:23b.

2. Our bodies are glorified (redeemed, 8:23) at the second coming (Philippians 3:21).

3. The cosmos is glorified also at the second coming (8:18-23).

CONCLUSION

This understanding of Romans does not require the availability of and a scholarly knowledge of extrabiblical Jewish writings. All it requires is an honest and persistent study of Romans itself, within the context of Scripture as a whole.

The so-called "New Perspective on Paul" and on Scripture as such is a rejection of one of the Protestant Reformation's "attributes" of Scripture, namely, the attribute of SUFFICIENCY. The Reformers rightly declared that Scripture is *sufficient*. This is true because of its *divine origin* (2 Timothy 3:16-17).

But there is more. The NPP's view is not just a challenge to the Bible's origin and nature, and to its sufficiency; it is also a denial of another of the attributes of Scripture, i.e., its *clarity*. How much "stuff" from outside the Bible do we really need in order to be able to understand it aright? The knowledge of such material may help with the understanding of details, but seldom if ever will it be needed in order to understand the basic meaning of Scripture.

In the final analysis, as one writer says, "At stake … is the very nature of revelation and its interpretation."

THE GOSPEL ACCORDING TO PAUL: A THEOLOGICAL OUTLINE OF ROMANS 1-8

From the beginning of my Seminary teaching in Fall 1967, I taught a course dealing with salvation by grace. It was based on Paul's explanation of the gospel in the first eight chapters of Romans. Thus I spent a lot of time analyzing this portion of Scripture. What follows is how I came to understand it then, and still understand it today. This appeared in print in the March 1976 issue of *The Seminary Review* (XXII:1), pp. 1-21. I have added a few notes along the way to reflect some later developments in my thinking.

PREFACE, 1:1-17.

A. What has the gospel to do with Paul? 1:1. It is his God-appointed task to preach it.

B. What has the gospel to do with the Old Testament? 1:2. It is in harmony with it. God has always had only one way of saving human beings. The Old Testament contains the gospel in promise, and it was through faith in the promise that people in Old Testament times were saved.

C. What has the gospel to do with Jesus Christ? 1:3-7. Christ is the subject or subject-matter of the gospel. The gospel is what Christ does to save us.

1. The gospel is the work of Christ FOR US, vv. 3-4. This is not a reference to the two natures of Christ (human and divine), but a reference to the two states of His incarnate existence: His humility and His exaltation. See the parallel in Philippians 2:5-11.

2. The gospel is the work of Christ IN US, vv. 5-7.

   a. The response demanded: the obedience of faith. This may be the obedience which consists of faith (says John Murray), or the obedience which results from faith (says J. W. McGarvey). I agree with McGarvey.

   b. The result produced: we belong to Jesus Christ, and we are made holy (saints).

D. What has the gospel to do with the book of Romans? 1:8-15. Romans is the most thorough explanation of what the gospel means for the Christian.

   1. Paul expresses his joy and concern for the Christians at Rome, and mentions his desire to come to Rome in person, vv. 8-12.

   2. Why does he want to go to Rome? He earnestly wants to preach the gospel in person to the Romans, but circumstances have thus far prevented it, vv. 13-15.

      a. Since he could not go to Rome and preach the gospel in person, Paul did the next best thing: he preached the gospel to them (and to us) in a letter. The book of Romans is Paul's own studied statement of the gospel, sent to the Romans in lieu of a personal visit. It is "a clear summary of the Christian faith" (says Charles R. Erdman). It is "the real chief part of the New Testament and the very purest gospel" (says Martin Luther).

      b. Romans shows us that "the gospel" includes more than the saving events themselves (the death, burial and resurrection of Christ). Indeed, it is the MEANING of these events for our lives which constitutes the bulk of Paul's presentation of the gospel. Romans is the expansion of the "for our sins" in 1 Corinthians 15:1-4.

E. What has the gospel to do with us? 1:16-17. We are its object. It is for us, for our salvation. It reveals to us the gospel truth, i.e., that salvation, in terms of being right with God, is by faith. (This is the theme of Romans, the gospel in a nutshell.) The "good news" of the gospel is not simply that we can be saved rather than lost. The good news is that we can be saved by FAITH rather than by works of law (Romans 3:28; Ephesians 2:8-10). So the main point of Romans is not primarily a contrast between sin and salvation, but a contrast between two possible ways of salvation: by grace through faith, or by law through works. Thus there are, in theory, two roads to God. But Paul's point is that one of these roads (works of law) has been thoroughly, permanently, and irreparably blocked by our sin. But God has graciously provided the alternate route (by grace through faith). This latter is now the only genuine road to salvation and way to God. But it is a way that is available to all, since the basic condition (faith) is one that all can meet.

1. The contrast is implied in verse 17, when Paul says that the gospel reveals a "righteousness of God." The implied contrast is between human righteousness (human works in fulfillment of some law) and divine righteousness (the gift of righteousness which God gives to us and on the basis of which we are declared righteous before Him). See Isaiah 61:10; Romans 3:21; 10:3; 2 Corinthians 5:21; Philippians 3:9.

2. Why is this called "gospel"—i.e., GOOD NEWS? Because the ONLY alternative to salvation by faith is salvation by works. If the latter were the only way to gain eternal life—if getting to

heaven depends upon our own righteousness (our works), then who could be saved? The outcome of such a system for sinners like us would be hopeless despair in this life and eternal damnation in the next. For who has lived perfectly in accordance with the law that applies to him or her? Who can plead innocent to the charge of transgression of the law? Not one. But here is the gospel, the good news: our salvation does not depend upon OUR righteousness, our ability to maintain sinless perfection. Our salvation rather depends upon a righteousness OF GOD earned by the works of Jesus Christ (verses 3-4) and bestowed freely upon all who put their whole-hearted trust in Him. In other words, salvation is by grace through faith, and not of works (Ephesians 2:8-10). On such gracious terms as these, who COULD NOT be saved? Here is a condition everyone can meet. Despair and doubt concerning our own salvation are replaced by happiness and hope and assurance, when we realize that our own personal salvation does not depend on our weakness but on God's strength. Is this not good news?

FIRST MAIN SECTION:
JUSTIFICATION BY (WORKS OF) LAW IS IMPOSSIBLE, BECAUSE OF THE UNIVERSAL SINFULNESS OF HUMAN BEINGS. 1:18 – 3:20.

The gospel is good news. But immediately after stating the grand theme of justification by faith (1:16-17), Paul plunges into a frightening discussion of mankind's sinfulness and condemnation. Why? Because this is the situation to which justification by faith is the only answer. The depth of sin from which Christ saves us reveals just how *good* the good news is. Unless one sees the terribleness of the wrath (1:18), he will not see the blessedness of the righteousness of God that is by faith (1:17).

So Paul's point in this section is that all people are sinners and stand under the wrath and condemnation of God. This not only shows us the misery of the condition from which we are saved; it also shows us the impossibility of being right with God by means of works of law.

The important element in this section is the LAW OF GOD. All human beings stand within the framework of God's law and must make some response to it. We cannot escape this decision. But within the framework of law, there are only two possible responses. One can keep the law, and thereby receive the blessings it promises; or one can break the law, and consequently pay the penalty it prescribes. Certainly any sane person would choose the former alternative and reject the latter. But herein lies the human predicament, as Paul shows so well in this section of Romans. When measured by God's law, ALL HUMAN BEINGS are found to be law-breakers who stand under the penalty of the law. This means that NO ONE can choose the alternative of keeping the law and therefore being justified by works of law. Therefore those who trust in the law (i.e., in their own ability to keep the law) are either deceiving themselves with a false self-righteousness or leading themselves into a hopeless despair.

I. **The sinfulness of the Gentiles, or heathen (those under General Revelation only) 1:18-32; 2:14-15.**

A. General Revelation. 1:18-21; 2:14-15. The special problem regarding the Gentiles or heathen is this: how do they know God's law? By what form of God's law can they be measured, found guilty, and condemned? The answer is that they know the law of God as it is given through GENERAL revelation (i.e., the revelation which is given to everyone *in general*). There are two main forms.

   1. God's revelation of Himself in and through nature. 1:18-21 (see Psalms 19:1ff.; Acts 14:17). God reveals Himself through the created universe, thereby placing on all people a duty to worship and serve Him.

a. The FACT of such revelation, verses 19-20. Ever since the time of creation, God has been revealing His eternal power and divinity through the created objects themselves.

b. The KNOWLEDGE which is received through such revelation, verses 19-21. Paul speaks of that which IS KNOWN and CLEARLY SEEN. He says unequivocally that all people KNOW GOD through the created universe. This includes all who have an awareness of created things, even the most primitive and isolated peoples on earth.

c. The DUTY which accompanies this knowledge and for which all are held responsible, verse 21. Paul condemns the Gentiles for failing to glorify God and give Him thanks. This is the fundamental LAW which they are obligated to obey, and there is no excuse for ANYONE who breaks this law (verse 20).

2. God's revelation of His law within and from human nature. 2:14-15. In this parenthesis to a discussion of the Jews, Paul indicates that the works of God's law are written upon the very hearts of all people. Though the Gentiles do not have the written law, in some way the law of God is built into the structure of human nature. Thus certain aspects of the law of God are "inwardly revealed" through "inward, natural promptings" (as J. W. McGarvey puts it). A general knowledge of what is right and what is wrong is somehow implanted in human nature. How? In virtue of the fact that man is created in the IMAGE OF GOD. See Ephesians 4:22-24; Colossians 3:9-10. The renewed image, and thus by implication the original image, includes a kind of KNOWLEDGE. Romans 2 suggests that even in the unrenewed man, vestiges of this (ethical) knowledge remain. All human

beings know enough to be without excuse (Romans 1:20), enough to be condemned for their disobedience.

B. General Rebellion. 1:18, 21-32. The question now is, how have the Gentiles responded to this law? Have they obeyed it or rejected it? The answer is the latter: they have rebelled against it. The rebellion takes two forms.

    1. The UNGODLINESS of men, or the reversal of their proper relationship to God. 1:21-23, 25. A willfully darkened understanding of the available true knowledge has led to false speculations about God and the substitution of idols for the true and living God.

    2. The UNRIGHTEOUSNESS of men, or the reversal of their proper relationships among themselves. 1:24, 26-32.

        a. There is a causal relation between ungodliness and unrighteousness. The former naturally leads to the latter.

        b. The emphasis is on the unnatural character of sin. Homosexualism is condemned. R. C. H. Lenski says, "Let go of God, and the very bottom of filth will be reached. Even the most unnatural will be called quite natural.... . The moment God is taken out of the control in man's life the stench of sex aberration is bound to arise.... . Without God, sex runs wild."

        c. Verse 32 shows the depth of depravity: even though they know that God's judgment on such things is death, they do them anyway and applaud others who do the same. (Paul does not mean to imply that all men everywhere have reached the depths of depravity described here.)

C. General Rejection. 1:24, 26, 28. Because of their abandonment of Him, God's wrath (verse 18) and judgment are upon the Gentiles. He has abandoned them to the full consequences of their sinful desires; He leaves them to suffer the penalty of death.

1. "God gave them up" means more than mere permission yet less than causation. It is a deliberate decision of God to withdraw His restraint of sin in the lives of individuals.

2. "Reprobate" means rejected, worthless, unfit, unworthy of praise, not standing the test. When measured by God's law, which they DO know to some extent, the Gentiles do not stand the test. They are condemned sinners.

II. The sinfulness of the Jews (those under Special Revelation also), 2:1 – 3:8.

Besides their knowledge of God and His will through general revelation, the Jews ALSO had a specially revealed version of the law: the Old Testament. This raises a problem with which Paul now deals: did God give this law as a favor to the Jews, as a safe-guard against His wrath? Does the Jews' special position as possessors of this special revelation— symbolized by circumcision—mean that they will receive privileged treatment in the final judgment? NO!

A. The Jew receives no special favors because of his privileged possession of the specially revealed law. Where God's law is concerned, no matter in what form it is possessed, the principles of judgment are the same for all, Jew and Gentile alike. Where law alone is the standard of judgment, all alike are responsible to it. 2:1-16. (But remember: where law alone is the standard of judgment, all alike are condemned by it, because all have sinned against it. This is the very point. See 3:20. The possibility of being saved by works is hypothetical *only*. Here Paul is only stressing the EQUALITY of all before the law.)

1. God will not be partial to the Jews when it comes to judgment, as many Jews thought. God renders to each according to his works, whether he be Jew or Gentile. If you obey, you are saved; if not, you are condemned. That's just the way it is where LAW is "the name of the game," 2:1-11.

2. Why are no favors shown to the Jews? Because there is only ONE LAW, though revealed in different ways and in different degrees of clarity; and the required response to it is the same for Jew and Gentile: obedience. Just being in *possession* of the law in a special written form is no substitute for obedience, 2:12-16.

B. The Jews are condemned by the very law they glory in, 2:17-29.

   1. The Jews' pride in—even TRUST in—the Old Testament law, 2:17-20, 23.

   2. The Jews' transgression of the law (and thus their condemnation by it), 2:21-24.

   3. The standard of judgment under a system of law is whether one keeps or breaks that law, not whether one bears the symbol of the law (in this case circumcision) or not. Once one commits himself to being right with God by the law, his only justification is to KEEP the law. There is no substitute. 2:25-29.

C. Paul vindicates God, who both gave a special revelation and yet condemned those who received it when they sinned against it, 3:1-8.

   1. Someone might object, What then is the advantage of being a Jew? Why has God taken so many pains with the Jews if they have no more privileges than the Gentiles? Isn't this a bit odd of God? No, says Paul. It is not that the Jews have no privileges at all. Above all else, they WERE given the spoken word of God, the very possession of which IS a definite advantage. 3:1-2. (See 9:4ff. for further discussion of this question.)

   2. The objector continues, So the Jews have the spoken word of God. Big deal. It didn't do them any good. They didn't keep it. They were unfaithful, and God condemns them. Doesn't this mean that God has failed in His purpose or has somehow prove unfaithful? NO, says Paul. Even if all the Jews should reject God and He should condemn them all, He is still righteous. For every

unrighteousness of man all the more by contrast shows the righteousness of God. 3:3-4.

3. But if our sin thus enhances His glory, why should He punish us? Oh, what a wicked thought, says Paul. Away with it! Whoever thinks such blasphemous things deserved to be damned. 3:5-8.

III. The sinfulness of all men, 3:9-20.

A. As declared by the Old Testament itself, 3:9-18.
   1. The Old Testament testifies to the universality of sinfulness, 3:9-12.
   2. It also tells us something of the awful depth of human corruption and depravity, 3:13-18.

B. As declared by the very nature of the law, 3:19-20.
   1. The law brings judgment upon all, 3:19.
   2. The law justifies no one, 3:20a.
   3. The law only shows us how sinful we are, 3:20b.

CONCLUSION

The purpose of this first main section has been to drive home to all of us the utter hopelessness and helplessness of our situation as breakers of the law. After all, there are only two possibilities open to us under law.

A. We can keep the law and escape the penalty. But this is impossible, for we are already sinners, or lawbreakers.

B. Or we can break the law and pay the penalty. This is the dreadful alternative, but this is where we actually stand in reference to the law. When we depend on our own abilities and our own righteousness, we cannot help being condemned.

Awareness of our desperate condition leads us to cry out to God, "Is there no alternative to your law? Deliver me from the curse of the law, or I die!" God answers, "For Me, there is no alternative; BUT for you there is! I, the Great Lawgiver, must abide by the terms of My own law. I must apply the penalty which My law demands. But at the same time, I offer you an alternative to My law: I offer you *My grace*, My pardon, an escape from the law and its penalty."

How can God do both? The answer is in Romans 3:21-5:21.

SECOND MAIN SECTION:
JUSTIFICATION BY FAITH. 3:21-5:21.

The apostle has established the fact of the universal sinfulness and condemnation of all human beings. All people are guilty; they stand in a wrong relationship to God's law. The fact of guilt raises the problem of justification. How can men be justified, or brought back into a right relation with God's law? Can a person perhaps work himself back into a proper relation to this law? Perhaps with a little extra effort, we can exert ourselves "above and beyond the call of duty" in the Christian life. Is this possible? NO! According to the parable of the unprofitable servant (Luke 17:7ff.), EVERY good work we can do is already owed to God (required by His law) and therefore cannot be used to pay the debt for past sin. This is why WORKS CANNOT JUSTIFY.

What possibilities are left, then? How can God justify us, or treat us as if we had never sinned, or treat us as if we had actually paid our deserved penalty? How can we escape the wrath and condemnation of God? Does any provision of the law allow a sinner to go unpunished? NO! If we are to be justified, we must come outside the framework of law and into the framework of grace. This is the point of this present section of Romans, as summed up in 3:28: We are justified by faith APART FROM works of law.

IV. God's way of justifying sinners is explained, 3:21-31.

A. We are justified by faith, 3:21-23. This is the gracious alternative to the unattainable justification by works.

1. Justification is a legal term and refers to the verdict pronounced by the judge. A person is justified if he or she is pronounced NOT

GUILTY by the judge. Of course, we ARE guilty; and this is the wonder of grace: the judge declares us NOT GUILTY anyway, and treats us just as if we had never sinned.

    a.   [This is a 2018 amendment to the previous paragraph. "Declared not guilty" is how I first learned to define justification; many still define it this way. I have changed my explanation thus: Yes, justification is the declaration of a judge regarding the defendant before him, but what he declares is this: "NO PENALTY FOR YOU!" And if the person is actually guilty and deserving of penalty, once justified, the judge treats him or her *just as if he or she has already paid the deserved penalty.*]

    b.   [I believe this slight change in the meaning of justification is more consistent with the actual *basis* of it, namely, Jesus's payment of that penalty in our place, as the next verses show.]

2. No rule of law provides for such justification of sinners. It is "apart from law" (3:28).

    a.   There is no article before "law." It is not just apart from the Old Testament law, but apart from law as such.

    b.   The preposition "apart from" carries an absolutely disjunctive force. Our justification has NOTHING to do with law. (This means that Luther's *sola* was not so much an addition to the text as it was an exposition of the text.)

3. We are justified by a righteousness which comes FROM GOD. It is a God-given righteousness, not a self-originated one. "My hope is built on nothing less than Jesus's blood and (Jesus's) righteousness." See Philippians 3:9; also Romans 1:17; 10:3; Isaiah 61:10. Luther's comment on Romans 1:1 says, "For God does not want to save us by our own but by an extraneous righteousness which does not arise on our earth but comes from

heaven. Therefore, we must come to know this righteousness which is utterly external and foreign to us. That is why our own personal righteousness must be uprooted."

4. "Justification by faith" means that this righteousness which justifies us is received by faith in Jesus Christ, instead of and apart from works we do or fail to do. The gift of righteousness is given not to the Pharisee who trusts in himself, but to the publican [tax collector] who puts all trust in God alone. Now, what is this faith that is able to appropriate the righteousness of God (something which all the works in the world cannot do)? It involves two things:

   a. Assent: a judgment of the mind regarding the truth of a statement, a belief that something is true. Cf. John 11:27; Romans 10:9; Hebrews 11:3.

   b. Trust: a decision of the will regarding surrender to a person. This is more than intellectual judgment; it involves commitment or surrender of yourself and what is in your power into the hands of someone else. It is an ATTITUDE of confidence and trust in another person. It is not just believing THAT; it is believing ON or believing IN. Cf. John 3:16; Acts 16:31; 2 Timothy 1:12.

5. This way of saving sinners is not a new way, 3:21. It was foretold and foreshadowed in Old Testament times, when grace was practiced but veiled in preparation for its complete unfolding at the coming of the Messiah.

6. This way of salvation is universally valid because it answers to a situation that is universally identical: all have sinned, all have transgressed the law of God. 3:22b-23.

B. We are justified by His blood, 3:24-26 (5:9). How is justification by faith possible, in light of the requirements of God's law? The law requires that its transgressors be punished. Does justification by faith mean that God has simply relaxed the law and its requirements? Has God sacrificed His JUSTICE for the sake of JUSTIFICATION? The answer is a firm NO! He is both *Just* and *Justifier* (3:26). But how can He be both? How can He both justify sinners by withholding their deserved penalty, and at the same time uphold the sanctity of His own law which requires the punishment of sinners? The answer: only through Jesus Christ and His substitutionary death on Calvary. We are "justified by His blood," i.e., the death of Christ is the God-provided ground for justification by faith. Christ bore the penalty for our sins in our place. Thereby the law of God is upheld even though sinners are justified by their faith alone. Only because Christ has satisfied the requirements of the law for us can the law be removed as a means of justification (Romans 10:4).

1. Our sin raises a problem that is "fit for God." Why cannot God just sweep our sin under the rug and say, "I forgive you"? Why is the death of Christ necessary for our justification? The answer: because of the very nature of God.

   a. God is JUST. The law of God is the expression of His own nature; therefore sin against the law is a contradiction of the very nature of God. His justice therefore demands that sin be punished. That which contradicts the holiness of God is consumed by it. "Our God is a consuming fire," Hebrews 12:29.

   b. God is LOVE. If justice were all that needed to be satisfied, then hell would be sufficient. But the love of God seeks the salvation of His creatures.

   c. Here is the problem: God is love, and love desires our salvation; but God is also just, and justice requires our damnation. How can God do both? How can He punish the sinner and save him at the same time? How can He be both just *and* justifier?

2. God solves the problem raised by our sin with a solution that is "worthy of God." He justifies us by the blood of Christ. Jesus bore the penalty of the law, thus upholding the justice of the lawgiver; and He bore it FOR US, thus allowing God to justify us by faith alone. (Though justification is appropriated *in baptism*, it is appropriated through the one and only *means* of faith. See Colossians 2:12.)

   a. Christ is our *redemption*, 3:24. He paid the debt of eternal punishment which we owed because of our sins.

   b. Christ is our *propitiation*, 3:25. Propitiation is "the turning away of wrath by an offering." Christ satisfied the wrath of God by taking the penalty of sin upon Himself. He bore the full force of God's wrath against sin.

   > *"Many hands were raised to wound Him;*
   > *none were interposed to save.*
   > *But the deepest stroke that pierced Him*
   > *was the stroke that justice gave."*

   c. Christ is our *substitute*. He satisfied the wrath of God not for His own sins, but for ours. To say that Christ bore our sins means that He bore the punishment for them. See 1 Peter 2:24; Isaiah 53; Galatians 3:13; 2 Corinthians 5:21. Christian friend, your sins have already been punished in Christ. This is how God can look at you, a sinner, and say "I forgive you"— and still be just.

3. Let us not forget that this solution to the problem of sin is provided by God Himself. "God set Him forth," says Paul. The

propitiatory atonement is the gracious provision of the wisdom and love of God. See 1 John 4:10.

C. We are "justified freely by his grace," 3:24.

    1. Our justification was purchased at infinite cost to God, i.e., the blood of the blameless lamb. Cf. Acts 20:28; 1 Peter 1:18ff.

    2. But justification is free to us. It is a matter of grace, not law.

        a. We do not earn it or deserve it. It is a gift, a handout. God's love, not our works, solved the problem of sin. The righteousness which justifies us is no more our own that the sins which Christ took upon Himself were His own: 2 Corinthians 5:21.

        b. Since it is free, we can do nothing at all in payment for it. Nothing we do is a payment for our forgiveness. To think so would be to doubt the efficacy of Christ's blood! Implications:

           (1) The believer has a marvelous freedom from fear and concern regarding his salvation. There is no price tag on salvation; i.e., our salvation does not depend on our ability to perform a certain amount of good works. Here is the source of great joy and relief and peace. This is true Christian freedom.

           (2) We learn to see our works, our Christian life, our conformity to the law, in a different light. Our obedience is not an effort to earn something we do not have as yet, but rather is an expression of thanksgiving for something already ours as a free gift.

    3. "Justified by grace" and "justified by faith" are compatible, because faith is a gracious condition and not a meritorious work. See Romans 4:16; Ephesians 2:8-10.

D. Implications of the doctrine of justification by faith, 3:27-31.

1. There is absolutely no reason for anyone to boast regarding his salvation, 3:27.

2. We are not justified by a combination of faith and works of law, 3:28. Mercy and merit do not mix.

3. This one way of justification applies to Jew and Gentile alike, 3:29-30.

4. This way of justification is not destructive to the law, but in fact allows the law to do its proper work, 3:31. Here Paul is anticipating the criticism that if we are justified by faith, we can just ignore the law and live as we please. (To this Paul says NO! in 6:1ff.) So how does this doctrine of justification by faith establish the law and allow it to do its proper work?

   a. It honors the Christ who fulfilled the law.

   b. It frees the law from a burden it was not intended or able to bear: that of justifying sinners. It was intended to show us that salvation is not of ourselves. When we believe in Christ, we are therefore acknowledging that the law has done its work.

   c. Only the believer who has been regenerated is enabled truly to keep the law as a rule of life (not as a means of justification).

V. Old Testament confirmation of the principle that justification is by faith and not by works of law, 4:1-25.

A. The outstanding proof and example of this principle: Abraham, 4:1-8. The Scriptures clearly say (Genesis 15:6) that he was justified by faith and not by works of law. The Psalms confirm this principle; see Psalms 32:1-2.

B. Those who imitate Abraham's FAITH are members of his family and recipients of God's promised blessings, 4:9-17.

   1. Abraham's faith, not his circumcision, is all that mattered as far as his justification was concerned. He is likewise the father of all who BELIEVE, whether they are circumcised or not, 4:9-12.

2. Abraham was not justified because of his relationship to any law, but because he believed in God and His promises, 4:13-17. Likewise the true descendants of Abraham and the sure heirs of the promises of grace are those who trust in the gracious God and not works of law.

C. The character of Abraham's faith: he gave God the glory, and rested completely on God's faithfulness and power to fulfill His promises, even it this meant doing what seemed to be impossible, even to the point of raising the dead. 4:17-22. See Hebrews 6:13ff. His faith was focused upon "God, who gives life to the dead." See Hebrews 11:11-19. For the fulfillment of the promise to Abraham, see Galatians 3; Acts 13:28ff.

D. Those who believe like Abraham will be justified like Abraham, 4:23-25. We must give God the glory, and be absolutely confident that God can and will keep His promises to us.

1. God's promises to us involve the resurrection of our dead souls (Ephesians 2:1-5) and the resurrection of our dead bodies (Romans 8:10-11). The blessings of *this* life depend on the former, of the *next* life on the latter.

2. How do we know that God CAN and WILL keep these promises? What is the basis for our faith? The RESURRECTION OF JESUS CHRIST. See Ephesians 1:19-20.

3. The focus of our faith is "God, who gives life to the dead." See Romans 4:24; 10:9; 2 Corinthians 1:9; 1 Peter 1:21; Colossians 2:12.

4. When is this faith exercised?

   a. At our baptism. Colossians 2:12.

   b. Throughout our life. Ephesians 1:13-14; Romans 8:10-11; 1 Peter 1:3-5; 2 Corinthians 5:1ff.; Philippians 3:10.

E. Thus, after the pattern of Abraham, the faith that justifies us is a faith and confidence in the ability of God to keep His promises, and not in our own ability to keep the law. The former gives glory to God; the latter gives the glory to ourselves.

VI. The blessed results of justification by faith, 5:1-11.

The results? Nothing less than "blessed assurance," "the hope of glory." Paul's point here is that justification by faith is a firm ground for confident hope, because it assures us that the love of God which provided the unspeakable gift for us WHILE WE WERE HIS ENEMIES will not fail us NOW THAT WE ARE HIS FRIENDS.

A. Justification, which is a change in our relationship to God (from wrath to peace), is a firm basis for hope (confident expectation) of eternal life. 5:1-2.

B. Even misfortunes are sources of hope and are not signs of God's disfavor, 5:3-4.

C. How justification (the change in our relationship to God) gives a basis for confident hope, 5:5-10.

1. The Holy Spirit makes us conscious of the love of God, 5:5.

2. God showed this unqualified love toward us while we were yet His unreconciled, sinful, helpless enemies, 5:6-8.

3. If God would do that for us while we were His enemies, we can have every confidence that He will do even more for us now that we are justified and reconciled, 5:9-10. When God first showed His love to us, we were His enemies. But now we are reconciled to Him. Will not God save those at peace with Him, if He went to the extremity of dying for His enemies? Will not His love suffice to make the less radical change which remains? Can God's love for His friends be less that His love for His enemies? If the love of God could span the vast chasm between wrath and grace (wherein we now stand), we are sure that this same love can span

the relatively smaller chasm between grace and glory. And just as surely as we did not span the first chasm ourselves by any works of our own, neither will the second be spanned by our works. God spans them both by His grace, and we cling to this grace by our faith.

D. We can only rejoice and praise God, 5:11. Our hope can be as strong and as unqualified as God's love. To doubt our salvation is to doubt the love of God.

VII. The triumph of grace over sin, 5:12-21.

The thought of this passage is summed up in this statement by A. I. Hobbs: "What, without our will or consent, we lost in the first Adam, we have regained or shall regain in the second Adam, without our will or consent." The purpose of God is not thwarted by sin. Christus Victor!

[The following notes are added in 2018. I am embarrassed at the brevity of the above comment on 5:12-21, but the truth is that in 1976 I was still not sure what to do with this passage! Since then it has become much more clear to me, and I will now add a couple of thoughts as to its meaning and purpose.

A. [First I will note that this text is most often cited as the Biblical basis for the doctrine of original sin, as if its main point is to say that Adam's sin has caused every one of his descendants (except Christ) to be born in a sinful state. Theologians disagree as to the severity of this state of sin, but most agree that this is Paul's main point. I have come to see that this interpretation of this text is obviously false, since the main emphasis here is not what we got from Adam, but what we got from Christ! Paul's point is similar to what Hobbs says (above). He is acknowledging that, yes, because of Adam's position as progenitor of the human race, through his sin all of his descendants WERE infected with serious sin-results, including death, condemnation, and sinfulness (vv. 15-19). But Paul's point is that these sin-results were *intercepted* and *set aside* for the whole human race by the foreknown grace-results of the cross of Jesus Christ: grace, justification, righteousness, life (vv. 15-19). The sin-results were canceled and never reached their target! No one is actually born in a state of original sin; we are all born in a state of *original grace!* See chapter 16 in my book, *Set Free! What the Bible Says About Grace.*

B. [What is this text doing here, anyway, at this point in the flow of Paul's thought? What does it have to do with what comes before and/or after it? Actually, it should be included under point III. above, "The blessed results of justification by faith," – 5:1-21! I believe that this section on original grace is a continuation of Paul's *application* of the justification-by-faith doctrine, i.e., that it gives us *assurance* of salvation. How does 5:12-21 establish our assurance even further than 5:1-11? Like this: All that Paul has said up through 5:11 is affirming that everything we need for justification, eternal life, and assurance thereof is all the result of something done BY ONE MAN, indeed, by ONE ACT of that one Man—the substitutionary death of Jesus on the cross. I.e., we are being asked to place our complete trust for our eternal future in *one act of one man!* And not just for me as one individual, but for anyone who will accept it! Isn't this asking a bit much? Can one act of one man have this kind of universal, eternal consequences? But wait—haven't we already seen this happen once—i.e., one act of one man, *ADAM,* affecting the eternal existence of the whole human race? Yes, that's what *would* have happened, if it had not been for the one act of the one *God-man, JESUS,* who is able to do whatever it takes to *cancel out* everything brought about by Adam, and MUCH MORE (vv. 15, 17)! The "much more" means that Christ has not only canceled out the results of Adam's sin, but also the personal sins of those who accept His works in faith. Yes: *Christus Victor!*]

THIRD MAIN SECTION:
SANCTIFICATION OF LIFE BY THE HOLY SPIRIT.
6:1 – 8:39.

In Romans 1-5 Paul has taught the doctrine of justification by faith, not by works of law. In the next three chapters he shows how this also involves sanctification or holiness of life. Here he says that the person who is justified by faith is also under obligation to live for Jesus, and he shows how such a life is possible through the Holy Spirit.

I. Paul answers objections to the doctrine of justification by faith, 6:1 – 7:25.

The objections are to the effect that if we are not under law but under grace, then we are under no obligation to obey God. Wrong, ways Paul. We *are* obligated to live a holy life.

A. The first objection, 6:1-14.

1. It would seem that the nature of grace encourages us to sin, 6:1. (See 5:20-21.)

2. The answer: whoever says this does not know what it means to be *united with Christ*. Union with Christ, initiated in baptism, means union with His death and resurrection. As Christ died to sin and rose to a new life, so do we when we are baptized into Him, 6:2-11.

3. Therefore, because we now have a new life, to continue in sin is a moral contradiction which we must strive to avoid, 6:12-14.

B. The second objection, 6:15 – 7:6.

1. If we are not under law, then we may sin as we please, 6:15.

2. The answer: whoever says this does not understand what it means to be free from the law. Freedom from law is not freedom from obedience. We are still servants or slaves, but now we have a new master whom we must serve with even greater devotion, 6:16-23.

3. Being released from the law, we obey our new master from an inward compulsion (i.e., loving gratitude) and not from the outward necessity of the letter of the law, 7:1-6.

C. The third objection, 7:7-25.

1. The law must be sinful, then, 7:7a.

2. On the contrary, the law is good, and I am sinful. The law simply reveals my sinfulness, 7:7b-13.

3. The Christian life is a continual struggle between the still-present sinful desires of the flesh and the inward desire to obey God's holy law. This inner conflict will persist until the day of final deliverance from this present body, 7:14-25.

II. Life in the Spirit. 8:1-30.

We are under obligation to live a holy life, but it seems to be a losing battle. How can we overcome ourselves and conform to God's will? We do so, progressively, through the guidance and power of the Holy Spirit within us. Despite the inner contradictions in this life, if the Spirit dwells in us now, we still have confident hope of eternal life.

A. The indwelling Spirit transforms us from death to life, 8:1-13.

1. The Spirit re-orients us away from ourselves and toward God, effecting both the baptismal resurrection of our dead souls (v. 10) and the future resurrection of our dead bodies (v. 11), 8:1-11.

2. We must therefore yield to the purifying and life-giving power of the Spirit, 8:12-13.

B. The Spirit confirms our adoption as children of God, 8:14-30.

1. Those led by God's Spirit are sons and heirs of God, 8:14-17.

2. Amid present suffering, and in possession of the "first installment" of our inheritance (v. 23; see Ephesians 1:13-14), we wait patiently and confidently for our full salvation, 8:18-25.

3. Meanwhile the Spirit helps us in times of distress, 8:26-27.

4. Knowledge of God's eternal and unchangeable purpose to gather together a Christ-like family gives us confidence in any situation, 8:28-30.

III. The triumphant conclusion to the doctrine of justification by faith: what God has done for us in Christ because of His love gives us (believers) joyful assurance of salvation, 8:31-39. (See 5:11.)

(This ends the systematic statement of the gospel according to Paul. Chapters 9-11 form another unit [a return to the question in 3:1], and chapters 12-16 form a final unit giving some specific instructions concerning holy living.)

For a more complete outline and extensive detailed exposition, see my commentary on Romans, *The College Press NIV Commentary: Romans*, 2 volumes (College Press, 1996, 1998; over 1,000 pages). See the one-volume condensed version, with Terry Chaney, 2005, 557pp., with a CD containing the original two volumes. On the law and grace themes in Romans and elsewhere, see my book, *Set Free! What the Bible Says About Grace* (College Press, 2009, 401pp.), and *Saved by Grace: The Essence of Christianity* (The Christian Restoration Association, 2017), 128pp.

CALLED TO FREEDOM

This essay on the message of Paul's letter to the Galatians was originally published in the Spring 1994 issue of *Bible Teacher and Leader* (96/2), published by Standard Publishing as the teacher's version of the regular Sunday School quarterly. The lessons for that quarter were taken from Galatians. I wrote this essay at the request of the editor. Quotations from Scripture are from the New American Standard Bible.

We value few things more highly than freedom. Because we are creatures, our freedom, of course, can never be absolute. But because we are human beings made in God's image, certain freedoms are ours by right and are necessary for the full expression of our humanness.

Some of these freedoms are external. Many people live in free countries where they are guaranteed free speech, free assembly, and freedom to choose their religion and their government. As important as these may be, the really significant freedoms are internal. We are not truly free until we are free from such bonds as anxiety, fear, falsehood, frustration, doubt, guilt, hopelessness, and meaninglessness. These are the things that bind our spirits.

Paul's letter to the Galatians is about the latter kind of freedom. "It was for freedom that Christ set us free," he says. "For you were called to freedom, brethren" (5:1, 13). Exactly what is Paul talking about, and what does this mean for Christians living today?

I. FREEDOM IN GALATIANS

The Galatian letter is Paul's response to a specific problem that faced the early church, especially in Galatia. The problem focused on the role of the law of Moses in the Christian's life. It was not a question of choosing between Moses and Christ; all agreed that we must become Christians. The question had to do with *how* one becomes a Christian. Exactly what is required for those who want to profess Christ and receive His salvation?

One group of converts from Judaism were unable to make a clean break with the law of Moses. They were called the *Judaizers*. They went around teaching that in addition to faith and baptism (3:26-27), one must be circumcised in order to be saved (6:12; see Acts 15:1).

The Judaizers were guilty of two specific errors. First, they assumed that the law of Moses (in part, at least) is still binding in the Christian age. Second, they assumed that salvation (specifically justification) comes by means of such law-keeping. Paul refutes both falsehoods by declaring that the gospel of Christ is a call to *freedom*. It sets us free from the Old Testament law as a way of life, and it sets us free from law as such as a way of salvation.

The law of Moses itself was a source of bondage in two ways. First, Paul explains how the Jews' existence under the law was more like slavery than sonship, because their place in history excluded them from full possession of the blessings of God's grace. They lived in the childhood stage of God's overall plan of redemption, which in some ways was similar to existing in the bondage of slavery (4:1-7).

Second, contrary to God's own intention for the law of Moses, many Jews regarded it as the means of their salvation. They believed they were saved by keeping the law. This seems to have been true of the Judaizers, at least with regard to the command of circumcision. One problem with this, says Paul, is that you cannot stop with circumcision. If you are going to bind this part of the law of Moses upon us, you have to go ahead and require it all (5:3). Thus bondage replaces liberty (2:4), and we become "subject again to a yoke of slavery" (5:1).

Paul affirms, however, that Christians are free from the law of Moses in both senses. First, we do not live in that slave-like childhood age. We live in the age of full sonship, in which we have full possession of the inheritance given through Abraham to his Seed, Jesus Christ, and to those who become one with Him in faith and baptism (3:23-29). The law of Moses was for the former age, not the latter. We are free from the legal requirements of that law, such as circumcision.

Second, we are definitely free from the law of Moses as a way of salvation. In the midst of his discussion of whether we have to "live like Jews" (2:14), Paul sums up the essence of our freedom in Christ: "Nevertheless knowing that a man is not justified by the works of the Law but through faith in Christ Jesus, even we have believed in Christ Jesus, so that we may be justified by faith in Christ and not by the works of the Law; since by the works of the Law no flesh will be justified" (2:16).

II. CHRISTIAN FREEDOM TODAY

It is extremely important to see that the last point above has a far broader application than just one system of laws. Few Christians today feel any obligation to obey the Mosaic law, and even fewer think of it as a way of salvation. But the truth of Galatians 2:16 applies not just to the law of Moses, which is actually just one example of the general principle. The fact is that no one can be saved by successful obedience to *any* list of God's rules and commands, including those written on the heart (Romans 2:14-15) and even those recorded in the New Testament.

This is the very point of Christian freedom; the grace of Jesus Christ sets us free from law—any law—as a means of salvation. We are saved by grace through faith, not by keeping commandments of law. What follows is a brief discussion of three important aspects of this freedom.

A. Freedom from Depending on Law-Keeping

First, as intimated above, we are free from *depending on law-keeping* as a way of salvation. This is indeed a glorious freedom, because there is no more hopeless bondage than thinking our day-to-day obedience is the key to acceptance with God. Such slavery makes us victims either of deception or of despair. On the one hand, if a person really thinks he is good enough to be accepted by God in this way (like the Pharisee in Luke 18:11ff.), then he is deceiving himself. On the other hand, the person who thinks he has to be "good enough" for Heaven, yet knows he is not, will be filled with anxiety, doubt, fear, and despair. Either way one is in the bondage of law-depending (which is the essence of legalism).

The glory of the gospel of grace is that it frees us from the legalistic mind-set. It frees us from both self-deception and despair. In Christ we are free from law-keeping as a means of being right with God. "For Christ is the end of the law for righteousness to everyone who believes" (Romans 10:4). When we put our trust in Christ, we are confessing that we are *not* able to obey in a way that deserves Heaven; but grace frees us from worrying about it.

A serious error to be avoided here, though, is that somehow the grace of God frees us from our *obligation* to obey God's commandments. Such is not the case; indeed, it is impossible for creatures of God ever to be relieved of their obligation to obey their Creator and Lord. This distinction must be carefully maintained: Christian freedom is not freedom from law-*keeping*, but freedom from law-*depending*.

B. Freedom from the Law's Condemnation

The *reason* we are free from law-depending is that Christ's death has set us free from the *condemnation* of the law. This is the second aspect of Christian freedom.

Anyone living under law (in the sense of depending on works for salvation) must be ready to accept the consequences of *breaking* the law, namely, eternal punishment in Hell. Thus for unsaved sinners, to be under law means to be under its condemnation or curse.

Here is the wonderful truth about Jesus Christ: He has borne this condemnation or curse for us! When we accept Him as Savior and Lord and become united with Him, He sets us free from this curse. "Christ redeemed us from the curse of the Law, having become a curse for us"

(3:13). "There is therefore now no condemnation for those who are in Christ Jesus" (Romans 8:1).

C. Freedom from Legalistic Motives for Obedience

The third aspect of Christian freedom is that we are set free from *legalistic motives* for obedience to God's commandments. That is, we are free from the law as a taskmaster that forces us to obey—or else! Knowing that we are justified by faith, we can obey the law simply because we *want* to. (It is still true, however, that we *ought* to.)

The Christian life is work! It often takes great effort to live according to God's will. The Bible describes Christian living as taking a yoke, working in a vineyard, reaping a harvest, fighting a battle, bearing a cross, and other such wearisome exercise.

Why does anyone want to work so hard? Why should we persevere in good works? What motivates us?

Living under law, one is driven by the dual motives of fear of punishment and desire for reward. Everything depends on personal obedience. Hence one must obey in order to escape punishment or in order to gain the reward. One may actually hate the things that God's law requires a person to do; but like a sullen slave he or she does them to escape the whip of God's wrath. Such an attitude is true bondage.

The grace of Jesus Christ sets us free from such self-centered motives, and provides the basis for the truly Christian motivation of grateful love. Faith in Christ continues to work, but it works through love (5:6). Jesus said, "If you love Me, you will keep My commandments" (John 14:15). Freedom from false motives allows us to cultivate this grateful love, which is the strongest, least selfish, and most Christ-centered of all motives.

The point is that the grace of the gospel of Christ frees us to obey God solely from love. Because of grace we are free from the law's penalty, on the basis of what Christ has done. Jesus paid it *all*; nothing we do adds to His payment. Thus if our justification is secure by faith, we are free to work and obey Him out of selfless love. Our daily obedience is not some kind of payment that God extorts or demands in return for His saving favors. It is simply our way of saying "Thank You" to a Savior who has freely given us everything.

PART THREE

SAVED BY GRACE

LAW OR GRACE?

This is the presentation I gave at the 2013 National Preaching Summit, directed by Brother Dru Ashwell, sponsored by College Press, and held at the Indian Creek Christian Church in Indianapolis, IN. This is actually the second edition of this work, since the original edition had been presented at the Men's Clinic in Hillsboro, OH, in May 2009.

INTRODUCTION

My purpose here is to explain what we usually mean when we use the word "grace," especially in the context of salvation. Condensing this down to a single sermon or lesson is quite a challenge for me, since in my seminary course on grace I lectured on the subject for over thirty-seven hours; and when I wrote my book on grace, called *Set Free! What the Bible Says About Grace*, it took me over 400 pages to explain the subject. But here goes!

My outline here is built around the fact that we use the word "grace" in three main ways when we are talking about salvation. First, we speak of grace as the SOURCE of salvation, i.e., grace as an attribute of God. Second, we speak of grace as the MEANS of salvation, i.e., the grace system in contrast with the law system. The third way we use this word is to refer to the CONTENT of salvation, i.e., the "double cure" of justification and regeneration/sanctification.

Here is how I will try to get these points across. Throughout this lesson I will build upon the idea that every human being stands in TWO main relationships with God. On the one hand: We are all *creatures* (created beings), and as creatures we stand in relationship to God as our CREATOR. At the center of this Creator/creature relationship is LAW (law codes, law system, works of law). On the other hand, ever since Eden we are all *sinners*, and because we are sinners God wants to be our SAVIOR. At the center of this Savior/sinner relationship is GRACE (gospel, grace system, faith in Jesus Christ).

God's good news for Christians is this: "You are not under law but under grace" (Romans 6:14; see also Romans 3:28; Ephesians 2:8-10). Now we are asking, what does it mean to be under grace, and not under law?

I. GRACE – AS AN ATTRIBUTE OF GOD – IS THE *SOURCE* OF SALVATION.

The first way we use the term *grace* is when we are thinking of God as the *source* of our salvation. In this context, grace is one of the main attributes of God, that aspect of His nature from which our salvation flows. In Exodus 34:6-7 God said to Moses, "The LORD, the LORD God, compassionate and **gracious**, slow to anger and abounding in lovingkindness and truth, who keeps lovingkindness for thousands, who forgives iniquity, transgression and sin." It is this *gracious* aspect of God's nature that provides salvation for sinners. This answers the "WHY?" question: why does God want to save us in the first place?

Here we will remember that we stand in two main relationships with God. Basic to everything else is the fundamental fact of the Christian world view: God is our Creator (Genesis 1:1ff.). He created all things, including human beings. This puts us into an irreversible, unchanging relationship with God, i.e., the relationship of Creator-to-creature. What is the *nature* of God as manifested in this role as Creator? He is transcendent, infinite, omnipotent, all-knowing, all-holy, and all-loving. As our loving Creator He has given us a created universe filled with an abundance of unimaginable blessings (1 Timothy 6:17—He "richly supplies us with all things to enjoy").

One of the main blessings our holy and loving Creator has given us is His holy LAW. God's law is a *blessing*. As Paul affirms in Romans 7:12, "The law is holy, and the commandment is holy and righteous and good" (see Psalms 19:7ff.). We can think of God's law as an instruction book. It is our LAW CODE. Every human being, all the time, is under a law code which he/she is obligated to obey. Everyone's law code has a generic section that applies equally to all: the "moral law" that is written on the heart. Even pagans are subject to this "heart code" (Romans 2:14-15).

Through special revelation God has given various specific law codes that are adapted to those living in different times and under different circumstances. The first main one of these was the Law of Moses, given to the nation of Israel in the Old Covenant era. This law code is no longer applicable for anyone, including the Jews. It has been replaced by the New Covenant law code, inaugurated via the death of Christ and spelled out in New Testament Scriptures. The New Testament has hundreds of law commands that apply to the whole human race. The whole world is now subject to this New Covenant law code, even if they are not all aware of it.

An individual's law code, whichever one it is, is ALWAYS a part of his or her life. No one is ever without a law code. It is a part of our relationship to the Creator. Our obligation, as creatures, is to give 100% obedience to the law code that applies to us (which is now the New Covenant law code). This obligation never changes.

But there is another, entirely different way in which we relate to God. This is because we as human beings have chosen to *disobey* our law codes, beginning with Adam and Eve. We have chosen to SIN. And — the entrance of sin (disobedience to our law code) has put human beings into a wholly new kind of relationship with God: the relationship of SINNER to SAVIOR.

Unlike the Creator-creature relationship, the Savior-sinner relationship is not universal, automatic, and unchanging. God's offer to be our Savior is a gift; we must choose to accept it. Here is where GRACE enters the picture. Grace has always been an aspect of God's nature, but before sin entered, it lay hidden in the heart of His love. It simply was not needed until sin came. The entrance of sin activated God's latent grace. I.e., like mild-mannered Clark Kent going into the phone booth and emerging as Superman, God becomes SuperSavior!

Actually, the entrance of sin into the world brought about a double reaction within God's nature. As our HOLY Creator, the latent attribute of *wrath* has emerged like an erupting volcano. In the presence of sin, our holy God manifests a desire or intention—even a *necessity*—to condemn all sinners to hell for eternity. Because He is holy, He must give sinners what they *deserve*: eternal condemnation. But at the same time, as our LOVING Creator, in the presence of sin his love now manifests itself as *grace*. Because of his grace, God desires to *save* sinners; because of His grace, God must necessarily provide salvation for sinners. This is simply *who God is*, as a God of grace. As the HOLY God, He must give us what we deserve; but as the GRACIOUS God, He desires to give us the *opposite* of what we deserve. This is the essence of grace, the essence of God.

These two relationships with God (Creator/creature; Savior/sinner) can be illustrated by the difference between the role of *government* and the role of your *doctor* in your life. Just as government makes and enforces laws that we are obligated to obey, so is God as the Creator our LAWGIVER and JUDGE. See Isaiah 33:22 – "For the LORD is our Judge, the LORD is our Lawgiver"; and James 4:12 – "There is only one Lawgiver and Judge, the One who is able to save and to destroy." But at the same time, just as doctors deal with sickness, telling us how to get well and stay well, so does God as the Savior tell us spiritually-sick sinners how to become saved and how to stay saved.

This leads to our second main point. In this first point we have explained that grace is the *source* of salvation, since it flows from the depths of the very essence of God, who by nature is the God of grace. This means that grace explains *why* God *wants* to save us. In the next point we are asking the question of *how* God saves us, and the answer is the same: He saves us BY GRACE. I.e., grace is the way or means or method by which we are saved. Or, to use the word I prefer: we are saved by the *grace system*.

II. GRACE – AS A WAY OR MEANS OF SALVATION – IS THE *SYSTEM* BY WHICH WE ARE SAVED.

The New Testament word for grace is *charis*, or "gift." Because God is gracious, He wants to GIVE us the most precious and unimaginably valuable gift, namely, *eternal fellowship with Himself*. The question is HOW? Under what conditions may God bestow this gift on us? There are two possible systems by which salvation – this eternal fellowship with God – can be given by God and received by us.

A. THE LAW SYSTEM

The first is the LAW system, which is the system of *works*, or as Paul sometimes says, *works of law*. Let's remember for a moment the fact that our primary relation to God is Creator-to-creature. Leaving sin and grace out of the picture for now, let's just ask: how might we, as simple creatures, like Adam and Eve were when first created, qualify (be eligible for) eternal fellowship with God? The answer is easy! Just keep on obeying your law code! ALL of it! Every commandment of it! Never sin! Live a perfect life!

This is what Paul is talking about when he refers to "salvation by works." When Paul uses the terminology of works, "works" are "works of law" (Romans 3:20, 28; Galatians 2:16). I.e., "works" are actions done in response to your law code, whichever one you are under. Theoretically, as creatures we could live in perfect obedience to our law code. As a result we would be rewarded with eternal life: eternal fellowship with God. In this case we would enter heaven on the basis of our life of good works, our everyday obedience to the New Covenant law code.

Now here is a crucial point: THIS is what Paul means when he says "works." *Whenever* he uses the term "works," he means "works of law," deeds done in response to our law code, in response to the Creator's instructions on how to live a holy life, whether that response is good (obedience) or bad (sin). Romans 4:6-8 shows that "works of law" (3:28) includes "lawless deeds" or "sins." At the same time "good works" (as in Ephesians 2:10) means everyday obedience, doing God's will, obeying our law code, being holy as God is holy, living the Christian life.

Eternal fellowship with God achieved in this manner (i.e., by law-keeping, by how well we keep the commands of our law code) would be "salvation" by the law system. *The law system is the way of entering heaven based on how well you keep your law code.*

So here is the crucial question: how well do you have to keep your law code in order to enter heaven thereby? How *good* do you have to be? How good is "good enough"? The answer: 100%! Perfect obedience! So, as long as you have never sinned, you are perfectly safe under the law system. You do not have to worry about God's wrath; you do not need grace. You are justified by your works.

In case you are wondering who is actually under this "law system," the answer is: every human being, as a creature of the Creator. It goes with the creation relationship. Adam and Eve were under the law system before they sinned; they were still under the law system after they sinned. And if they remained under the law system, they were lost for eternity, because the law system is a means of eternal fellowship with God *only as long as one has not sinned.* Once one has sinned, even once, fellowship with God is lost, and the law system is impotent as a means of restoring that fellowship.

The problem, of course, is that *all have sinned* (Romans 3:23) and have thus ruptured our relationship with our Creator, and the law system is useless as a way of restoring that relationship. This is what the Bible means when it says that works of law cannot save sinners (Romans 3:20)! Here is an illustration: There is a certain "law code" for how to treat and care for your teeth so that they will remain healthy. We can call this the "tooth code." I.e.: brush and floss daily, see your dentist twice a year, don't chew on nails and unpopped popcorn kernels, and don't use meth! (When I was a child we sang this ditty: "Do you brush your teeth each morning and each night? If you'll surely do that, they will be all right." That was our tooth code!)

But what if you DISOBEY your tooth code? Your teeth will crack or decay and rot and get loose in your gums and start to turn black and fall out. Ewww! So NOW what can you do? You *could* go back to your tooth code, and *get serious* about taking care of your teeth. That's fine, BUT it won't save your rotten teeth. That will require a *totally different strategy or approach!*

It is the same with sin and salvation. Once your life has been infected with sin, just getting serious about your law code is not going to solve that problem. This is why God has provided another wholly different SYSTEM of salvation: the system of *grace*, which we will now consider.

B.   THE GRACE SYSTEM

When we as sinners accept Jesus Christ as Savior and obey the gospel, we are no longer under the law system, but have come under the grace system. This is the meaning of Romans 6:14, "You are not under law but under grace."

Here are two main things that happen to you when you sin and become a sinner. First, the law system of maintaining fellowship with God—ensuring heaven via how good you are—is now useless. Once your sins are "on the books," the law system just shuts down for you! No matter how hard you try to obey all the commands in your law code, it won't solve the sin problem. (Just like with your teeth: once they have rotted, no matter how hard and how often you brush them, they won't heal.) Likewise, as a sinner, no matter how many good works you can do, they cannot make up for your sins. Nothing you can do can ever make up for them.

The second thing that happens now that you are a sinner is this: you are now *eligible* for *grace*! You qualify for the grace system! You have the opportunity to enter into a wholly new and different relationship with God! Now, as a sinner, for *salvation* purposes you may enter into a relationship with God as your SAVIOR. In fact, this is now your only hope! You are still related to God as your Creator, but not for salvation purposes. God as Creator can take you to heaven only via the *law* method;

but that won't work for sinners. Now, you *must* come under the grace system in order to be saved.

How does the grace system work? How do we receive salvation under the grace system? Salvation is *accomplished* by Jesus Christ, and then *offered* to sinners. So how can we accept that offer?

Here is a crucial distinction in Paul's terminology. Under the law system you reach heaven by *works*, i.e., *works of law* (if you have perfect obedience). But under the grace system you reach heaven by *obedience to the gospel*. This terminology comes first from Romans 10:16, where Paul is explaining why the Jews in New Testament times were not automatically saved, as they thought they should be. Why not? Because, as the ESV rightly translates it: "They have not all obeyed the gospel." I.e., obedience to the gospel is the way sinners accept the offer of salvation. This is confirmed by 2 Thessalonians 1:8, where Paul says that when Jesus returns he will be "dealing out retribution to those who do not know God and to those who do not obey the gospel of our Lord Jesus."

This means there are *two kinds of commands* coming from God, and *two kinds of obedience* on our part. First are *works of law*, or how you respond to the CREATOR's *law* commands (your law code). Then comes *obedience to the gospel*, or following the SAVIOR's *instructions* on how to be saved. Thus both law and grace involve *imperatives* to be obeyed. Just as there are law commands, so also are there gospel commands. (The gospel includes not just gospel facts, but also gospel promises and gospel commands. "*Obedience* to the gospel" requires gospel *commands* to be obeyed.)

What are these gospel commands? They are quite familiar: (a) Believe on the Lord Jesus Christ. Mark 1:15; John 12:36; Acts 16:31. (b) Repent of your sins. Matthew 3:2; 4:17; Mark 1:15; Acts 2:38; 3:19; 17:30; 2 Peter 3:9; Revelation 2:16. (c) Confess Jesus as Lord and Savior. Romans 10:9-10. (d) Be baptized for forgiveness of sins and the gift of the Spirit. Acts 2:38; 22:16. These are not *law* commands, since they are not given to us by God in His role as Creator, telling us how to live holy lives in His presence. These commands are given to us by God in His role as Savior, telling us what we must do to be saved from sin.

Which system of salvation are you under? The law system, which is the case if your only relation to God is your relation to Him as your Creator? Then you are LOST. Or are you under the grace system, provided freely for you by God as Savior? Then you are SAVED. What does Paul say to you as a Christian? "You are not under law, but under grace" (Romans 6:14).

I will close this section with the illustration of two keys to heaven. In our area of Indiana some automobile dealers mail keys to area households, saying the key you receive MIGHT fit a new car in their showroom, in which case you will win the car! Now, think of heaven as a walled city having one gate, which is locked. You must have a key to get in. God offers each of us a choice of TWO keys to try in that lock, and he tells us in advance that only one key will work. BUT he also tells us in advance WHICH ONE will work, and which one won't. The LAW key, "works of law," will not open heaven's gate for sinners. The GRACE key, faith in the work of Jesus Christ, WILL open the door to heaven!

III. GRACE – IN THE BASIC SENSE OF A GIFT – IS THE *CONTENT* OF SALVATION.

We have asked the questions WHY? and HOW? Now we ask— WHAT? What is the grace that God gives to sinners? Once you decide to respond to the Savior's offer of salvation, and obey the gospel as instructed in the New Testament, what happens at that point? In that moment the gracious God gives you a gift package: the gift of salvation. You come up out of the baptismal water clutching this package. What's in it? GRACE! Thus we are saved *because of* grace, *by* grace, and *unto* grace.

Ever since the early 1960s I have been speaking of grace as God's "double cure" for sin. I found this expression in the old song, "Rock of Ages," where it calls upon Christ's death on the cross to "be of sin the double cure: save me from its guilt and power!" (Sometimes a different wording is used: "Save from wrath, and make me pure!" The meaning is the same.) The point is that when we are thinking of the content of the grace-gift that is received in the moment of salvation, it has two main parts, as follows.

A. GRACE AS JUSTIFICATION

The first and primary element in the grace package we receive in Christian baptism is *justification*, or the forgiveness of sins. Literally, justification is something that happens in a courtroom. You are the defendant—in fact, a *guilty defendant*, standing before the Judge. Justification is the Judge's declaration to you of His findings as to your status before the law. His declaration is this: "NO PENALTY FOR YOU!" As Romans 8:1 says, "Therefore there is now no condemnation for those who are in Christ Jesus." This is the essence of what it means to be justified.

The point is that by this judicial act, all the consequences of our *guilt* are immediately removed; our debt of eternal punishment in hell is considered paid in full. This is a legal change in our status; our relationship to the law and to the Lawgiver has been changed. It is not something that happens to us internally or subjectively; it happens externally, outside of us. Most specifically, becoming justified is a change that takes place in the mind of God. He no longer looks at us as owing the debt of eternal punishment in hell; He looks at us as having paid that debt and as being back in full fellowship with Him.

This gift of justification is possible only because of the atoning work of Jesus Christ. As our substitute He bore the wrath of God in our place; He paid the debt of punishment that we owe. Every sin is like an IOU, indicating that we owe God eternity in hell. Jesus paid all of these IOUs for us on the cross (Colossians 2:14). The package of grace we receive at baptism includes all these canceled IOUs.

This justification was not just a one-time act of God; it is also an ongoing possession, resulting in a sense of peace or assurance of salvation (Romans 5:1-11). That we are "justified by faith" means that we *became* justified or forgiven in that baptismal union with Christ, and that we continue to live in a *state* of justification or forgiven-ness. It is not just our sins that are forgiven; we are *forgiven persons.*

B.   GRACE AS REGENERATION

The second element in the grace package is what is usually called *regeneration*, or the new birth, or the new creation, or being raised up from spiritual death to new spiritual life. This is something that does happen *inside* of us; it is a change in our inner nature wrought as the result of the Pentecostal gift of the indwelling of the Holy Spirit (Acts 2:38). As soon as the Spirit enters our hearts and bodies in Christian baptism, He renews and regenerates us (Titus 3:5), as if He were a surgeon performing an operation on our hearts (see Ezekiel 36:26). So, just as we can use the imagery of the courtroom to define justification, we can use the imagery of the operating room to explain regeneration.

This regeneration or new birth is itself just a one-time act of healing or resurrection, but its result is on-going and lasts throughout the Christian life. This is true because the Holy Spirit who enters into us and regenerates us in baptism continues to indwell us, as the source of spiritual strength for *sanctification*. In this sense God's grace is constantly with us, working in us, changing us to become more and more holy as God is holy (Philippians 2:13; 1 Peter 1:15-16).

These two aspects of salvation – justification, and regeneration/sanctification – constitute the *content* of the grace-package we receive at the moment of conversion.

CONCLUSION

Here is something that is very important, something that we must never forget. As sinners, when we accept the gift of grace, we enter into a relationship with God as our Savior. We are now under the grace system of salvation. However, even as sinners saved by grace, we are also still creatures of the Creator-God. We are still in a Creator-to-creature relationship with God. This will never change! Thus we are still 100%

obligated to obey the New Covenant law code as a *way of life,* though not as a way of salvation.

We are no longer under the law *system.* I.e., we are no longer *seeking salvation* by means of our obedience to our law code. But we still have an absolute obligation to obey that law code – not to save ourselves by "living the Christian life," but just because *God is God!* He is still our Creator and our Lawgiver!

The blessing of grace is that God as our Savior has given us the POWER (through the indwelling Spirit) to put sin to death in our lives (Romans 8:13) and to obey the law commandments he has bound upon us as our Creator (Ephesians 3:16). This is what we will do if we love Him (John 14:15).

SAVED BY GRACE—NOT BY LAW: A DRAMA

At heaven's gate, when you are asked, "Why should we let you into heaven?" what will you say? What answer do you think God wants to hear? What is the right answer? Consider this story, which is a variation of a motif that has been developed many times before.

An honest, hard-working member of the community went to sleep one night and dreamed that he had died and was now standing in front of a large gate into heaven. He noticed a sign posted near the gate. It read, "ENTRANCE REQUIREMENT: 1,000 POINTS." There was an angel guarding the gate. The man walked up to the angel, and the following conversation ensued:

MAN: One thousand points, eh? That requirement seems pretty high. What about me? Do you think I have accumulated that many points?

ANGEL: Well, I don't know. Why don't you tell me what you have done, and tell me why you think you deserve to get in. Then, we will see how many points you have.

MAN: OK, I think I can do that. First of all, I lived a life of peace with my neighbors. I never caused any trouble with anyone. I was not mean; I never fought with or hurt anyone. In fact, I was always ready to help people if they were in trouble. I gave money to people who needed it. I donated to the Red Cross for flood relief. How's that?

ANGEL: That's very good! Now let me see. Hmmm. That's worth— ONE POINT.

Here the man became a bit pale, and began to perspire. But he went on:

MAN: I tried my best to keep the ten commandments. I never killed anyone. I was tempted many times to commit adultery, but I never did. I was faithful to my wife. I treated her very well. I never yelled at my kids. I never stole anything, or robbed a bank, or took stuff home from the office. I never cheated on my income tax. So what do you think? (Please, please, please … .)

ANGEL: That's all good also. I think we can give you two points for that. Now you have THREE.

The man looked as if he were about to go into shock, and he spoke rapidly with a sense of desperation:

MAN: Okay, I've got more! I went to a lot of churches during my life. I tried to go at least twice a year. I gave money to churches and other charities. In our town a church building burned down and I helped rebuild it. I never joined a church but I respected what they were doing. I believed in God and tried to think about Him and pray to Him sometimes, especially when I was outdoors fishing or playing golf. We always said grace at meals.

ANGEL: That's all really great. That's worth another five points. You now have a total of EIGHT.

The poor man's face sagged with hopelessness. His shoulders drooped, and he seemed resigned to his fate:

MAN: I may as well give up. At this rate there's no way I can ever get to 1,000 points, and convince you that I'm good enough to go to heaven.

Just then the man looked up and noticed a huge sign hanging above the gate into heaven. It had just one word on it: L-A-W. He asked the angel, "What does LAW mean?"

ANGEL: Oh, that's what we call this gate into heaven. It's the "Law Gate." We call it that because this is how you get into heaven here: by keeping the law of God, by obeying His commandments, by being good.

MAN: What do you mean? Do you mean that we have to keep the Law of Moses to go to heaven? I thought the Law of Moses was set aside by Christ.

ANGEL: No, that's not what I'm talking about. The whole thing about the Law of Moses misses the point completely, and a lot of people have misunderstood this. Let me explain. First, you have to distinguish between a law *code* or set of commandments, and law as a *system* for getting into heaven. Second, "law" as a way of getting into heaven relates equally to every law code and is not limited to the Law of Moses. It includes whatever law or set of commandments applies to any given person. Here's how it works.

1. God's law is everywhere. It is the original natural framework of God's creation. Just as God built the laws of physics into the material universe, so he built the laws of morality into our hearts. Law is just the way things are, and the way they ought to be. We are born into a universe of law.

2. All people in all times and places are under some law code, or some version of God's law. This always includes God's laws of basic morality; these never change. Even pagans who never heard of the Bible have God's law in this basic form. It's written on every human heart. See Romans 2:15.

3. If you had been a Jew living between Moses and Christ, the relevant law code would have been the Law of Moses. But even in the Old Testament times, not everyone was under the Law of Moses; and since Christ came, no one is. Not even the Jews.

4. Those of us who live in the New Testament age have the law commands and law requirements given to us in the revealed and inspired writings of the New Testament Scriptures.

5. Thus getting into heaven through the law gate does not necessarily involve the Law of Moses. It's a matter of the way you obey whatever law code you happen to be born under and live under.

MAN: Thanks for explaining that, but here's the question that's really bothering me. Can a person actually get into heaven by obeying the code of law commandments that applies to him?

ANGEL: This may surprise you, but the answer is YES— theoretically, at least. A person *can* get into heaven by law alone without any special help from God or from Jesus Christ. I have to tell you this. You see, the law system of salvation operates according to a strict set of rules that show you how to escape hell and get into heaven by keeping the law. If you will look over there just to the right of the Law Gate, you will see a small sign that reads thus:

> *"Keep the commandments, and escape the penalty.*
> *Break the commandments, and suffer the penalty."*

So there you are! Just "keep the commandments." That's all there is to it. It's as simple as that. This is how you can enter this law gate into heaven.

MAN: You mean I can earn one thousand points by keeping the laws that apply to me? By obeying the law commandments? But I only got up to eight points, and I didn't have much more to present on my own behalf!

ANGEL: Yes, you can earn a thousand points. But you can do it only by keeping all the commandments that apply to you *all your life*, and by *doing it perfectly*. You have to live a perfect life. You can't just keep a *Reader's Digest* condensed version of the law, such as the ten commandments or the sermon on the mount. Even every *thought* has to be perfect. Remember how Jesus said that lusting after a woman is committing adultery in your heart? Also every *word* has to be perfect. The New Testament says, "Let no evil word proceed out of your mouth." That's part of the law you must keep. Have you ever in your life said an evil word?

MAN: Well, yes, but not too many. I've said a lot more good words than bad!

ANGEL: Ah, yes—the old "balance scale" fallacy. Contrary to the belief of many, you cannot cancel out your sins or make up for them with your good works. Actually, it's the other way around. No matter how many good works you do, just one sin cancels them all out! One sin, and you lose! Break the commandments—even *one*, and you suffer the penalty. Remember James 2:10 and Galatians 3:10.

So, my friend, if we were to continue with the examination of your life, and expose your sins as well as your good works, you would realize that you don't even have *eight* points! Your sin has canceled even that! You actually have none at all. So even if you needed only one point to get into heaven, that would be canceled out by your sins.

MAN: Do you mean that no one can get through this gate into heaven unless he is perfect? But that's terrible! The Bible says no one is perfect! Romans 3:23 says that "*all have sinned*"! But that means ... that means ... no one will actually be saved by law, or law-keeping, or by being good enough. No one can be good enough to go to heaven. No one will ever deserve to go to heaven!

ANGEL: Now you get the point. Once you sin, no matter how hard you try, there's no hope of entering this gate. In fact, look here: do you see? It's padlocked! It has never even been opened. It has never been used, and never will be. No one will ever get into heaven through this gate because, as you have said, all have sinned.

MAN: But that's awful! How can anybody have any hope of going to heaven? How can anyone ever be saved? I thought God was a loving God! Whatever happened to His grace?

ANGEL: What? What did you say? Did you say **GRACE**? Well, my friend, if you want grace, you are in the wrong place; you are at the wrong gate into heaven. This is the LAW gate. Look around the corner of the wall there. Do you see down there a bit? There's another gate into heaven down there. That's the GRACE gate. See the big sign over it: G-R-A-C-E.

MAN: What do you mean? There are *two* gates into heaven?

ANGEL: Certainly. Whoever said there's just one? Didn't anyone ever tell you? Ever since sin came into the world, there have been two ways of relating to God. See Romans 6:23: "For the **wages** of sin is death, but the free **gift** of God is eternal life in Christ Jesus our Lord." "Wages" and "gift"—these are your choices. The first is law, the second is grace. Under the first you get what you have earned, what you deserve; under the second you get heaven as a free gift, not as something you have deserved. That's what these two gates are about. Where we are now is the gate for those who are living their lives under the law system; around the corner is the gate for those who are living their lives under the grace system. The only problem is, no one ever goes through this one. The only actual way that sinners can get into heaven is through the grace gate.

MAN: But how can that be? Is grace really that much different from law? How does the grace system work? How do you get into heaven through the grace gate?

ANGEL: Oh, they are different all right. Grace as a way of salvation goes by a completely different set of rules. If you were standing down there by the grace gate, you could see the small sign on the wall just to the right of it. Here's what it says:

> *"Keep the commandments, but suffer the penalty.*
> *Break the commandments, but escape the penalty."*

MAN: Wait a minute! "Break the commandments, but escape the penalty"? That doesn't sound fair! How can anyone break God's commandments and not have to suffer the penalty?

ANGEL: You are right—it isn't fair. Law is fair. If you want to be treated fairly on the day of judgment, stay under the law system. This law gate is where you want to be if you want God to be fair with you. Here's where you get "the **wages** of sin." But who really wants to get what they deserve on the day of judgment? Wouldn't you rather have grace? Grace gives you the very opposite of what you deserve. "Break the commandments, and suffer the penalty"—that's the law system, and that's what you deserve. But the grace system says, "Break the commandments, but escape the penalty." Of course it's not fair: *it's GRACE!*

MAN: Hey, that does sound awfully good! But what about the first rule of the grace system. You know, "Keep the commandments, but suffer the penalty." That *really* doesn't sound fair, either. But what's that all about? It seems so irrelevant, because we have already seen that no one ever keeps all the commandments. Everyone has sinned. So that part of the grace system doesn't really apply to anyone, does it?

ANGEL: Well, yes it does. In fact, it's the really absolutely essential part of grace. You see, there was one person who did keep all the commandments, one person who lived a perfect life. This rule is intended to apply only to Him.

MAN: Who was that?

ANGEL: Jesus Christ, of course. He never sinned. And you know what else He actually did, don't you? He suffered the penalty for sins. He kept the commandments for Himself, and He suffered the penalty for the sins of the whole world. Think about 2 Corinthians 5:21, "He [the Father] made Him [Jesus] who knew no sin to be sin on our behalf, so that we might become the righteousness of God in Him." This is grace: we each get the opposite of what we deserve. Jesus took the opposite of what He deserved, so that He could give us the opposite of what we deserve. This means that Jesus has traded places with us. On the cross He took what we deserve, so that on the Judgment Day we may actually get what He deserves.

MAN: Do you mean that we don't need 1,000 points to get through the grace gate?

ANGEL: That is correct. In fact, you don't need *any* points. Jesus has already taken care of your "entrance fee," as it were. There is a cost for getting into heaven, but Jesus paid it for you! To you, it's free. That's the whole point of grace. You don't get into heaven because you deserve it. You deserve the wages of sin, which is eternal death in hell; but Jesus paid everything you should have paid, and He gives you everything that He deserves. That's grace.

MAN: Well, that sounds good to me! I'm going to go over there to the grace gate right now!

ANGEL: Wait a minute—I'm so sorry! I'm afraid that will be impossible. It's too late for that. You are already dead, remember? Anyone who wants to get into heaven through the grace gate must get in the grace line while he is still alive. Do you remember all the opportunities you had to become a Christian while you were alive? But you kept putting it off. Now it's too late.

As the angel spoke, the man felt his feet getting hot. He looked down to see that he was standing on a trap door. Just as he started to utter a tragic scream, the angel pushed a nearby button; and the man fell through the trap door into outer darkness and the agonies of hell.

But then the man woke up! Remember, this was a dream. His bed was soaked with perspiration. As soon as he stopped shaking he called the preacher in the Bible-believing Church of Christ in his town, and said he was ready to talk about becoming a Christian and getting in the grace line to heaven. They talked, and the man came to faith and repentance, confessed Jesus as his Lord and Savior, and was immersed into Christ and became a faithful member of the church.

A few months later he had another dream. He dreamed he had died and that he was standing in front of the grace gate into heaven. At that gate stood Jesus Himself, who looked kindly at the man and spoke gently to him:

JESUS: Why should I let you into heaven?

MAN: I have only one thing to say to that: *"Just as I am, without one plea, but that Thy blood was shed for me."* Wait! I thought of something else: *"Nothing in my hand I bring; simply to Thy cross I cling."*

JESUS (looking directly into the man's eyes with His own loving gaze): That's what I wanted to hear! I know you, My friend!

Then Jesus put His arms around the man, and embraced him warmly, and told him to enter the grace gate into the glories of heaven.

At that point the man woke up from this second dream, and his eyes were filled with tears of joy. Then he turned over and went back to sleep in a state of perfect peace and assurance.

WELL—that's the end of the story; now here are the facts:

ONE. If you are not a Christian, you are in the law line, under the law system, on your way to the law gate. And you will need your 1,000 points to get through that law gate—that *padlocked* law gate— into heaven. On Judgment Day you will be judged by the rules of law; you will have to show God that you *deserve* to go to heaven.

What does this mean for you now? It means you have every reason to be filled with terror and dread. Why? Because you know that on the day of judgment you will get what you deserve; that is the nature of the law system. When God says, "Why do you think you deserve to go to heaven?", you will have to produce your 1,000 points. So all your life you are haunted by the prospect of having to show God why you deserve to go to heaven and not hell, and you know that will be impossible.

TWO. But if you are a Christian, everything is different! As Paul says in Romans 6:14, *"You are not under law, but under grace"*! You are under the grace system; you are in the grace line; you are on your way to the grace gate. On Judgment Day you will stand before the grace gate into heaven and be judged by the rules of grace.

And what does this mean for you now? It means you are not worried, because you know that Jesus paid your entrance fee into heaven, and the gift of eternal life is waiting for you. You don't have to accumulate 1,000 points, or convince God that you deserve to get into His heaven. It's like having a ticket to heaven in your pocket now.

THREE. Just knowing you are in the grace line makes all the difference in the world as to your peace of mind, your Christian life, and your service to Christ. It affects your whole state of mind concerning life, death, and the judgment.

Are you ready for the Judgment Day? Do you have your ticket? Do you have your answer ready for when God asks you why He should let you into heaven? You can say YES to these questions! You can sing "Blessed Assurance," not "Blessed Possibility"! You can sing, "When the roll is called up yonder, *I'll be there!*"

FOUR. In view of all of this, which line would you rather be in?

FIVE. If you are not a Christian, make the switch now. Get out of the law line, and get into the grace line. If you are a Christian, stop living and thinking and worrying as if you were still in the law line.

HAVE WE LEARNED TO *THINK* IN GRACE?
AN AID FOR SELF-EXAMINATION

In Romans 6:14-15, Paul says we Christians are "not under law, but under grace." I.e., we are not under the law system as a way of salvation; we are under the grace system. We know that we are still obligated to obey God's law commands, but we realize that we are not saved by achieving a certain level of obedience to those commands. Rather, we are saved by the grace of God, through our sincere trust in the redemptive works of Christ. As believers we exist in grace; we live in grace; we act in grace.

But do we THINK in grace, i.e., in terms of grace? Are our thought patterns consistent with being saved by grace? In a real sense, law and grace are *attitudes, states of mind, mind-sets, mentalities*. One's whole spiritual and mental approach to life and salvation will be measured either in terms of law, or in terms of grace. We can live either with a *law mentality*, or with a *grace mentality*.

Many Christians are still living AS IF they were under law. But this is not good. Even if we are saved, we cannot experience the joy of our salvation if we are still trapped in the law mentality.

How can we tell whether we are still laboring under a law mentality, or whether we have learned instead to "think in grace"? One way is to examine how we think about certain things. I.e., what do we think about ourselves? About our works? About God's law? About the way of salvation? About God Himself? Here we need to take some time for self-examination.

I. What is your estimate of YOURSELF, i.e., of your personal worthiness and ability before God?

A. In general, the LAW-minded person has a high opinion of himself, and considers himself to be quite worthy of salvation and not far from what God requires. One who thinks in terms of law has a superficial view of his personal sin and of his weakness before God. He is the "good moral man" who thinks he deserves heaven if he doesn't drink or cuss or fool around. He is rather proud of himself.

B. The GRACE-minded person, on the other hand, knows he is a sinner, and that he is unworthy of salvation. He has a keen sense of his sinfulness and of his need for mercy. He knows his weaknesses and pleads for help. He acknowledges that the good he does is by God's grace working in him – that he does good because he is saved, not that he is saved because he is good. He thinks like the tax-collector, not the Pharisee (Luke 18:9-14); like the prodigal son, not the elder brother (Luke 15:11-32); like the Apostle Paul after his conversion, not before (1 Timothy 1:12-16).

C. How are you thinking? Are you resting your confidence in your own ability to keep God's law, or are you resting your confidence in God's ability to keep His promises?

II. What is your attitude toward GOD'S LAW?

A. Quite often, the LAW-minded person actually *hates* the law, but obeys it outwardly through fear of going to hell, or simply through a desire to go to heaven. One who thinks in terms of law would rather disobey if he could get away with it. He keeps the law, but for selfish reasons. There is outward conformity, but inward rebellion. The LAW-mind is an unwilling slave to the law.

Martin Luther summed it up well: "What, then, is the difference before God between one who does evil, and another who wants to do evil but does not do so only because he is restrained by fear or enticed by the love of some temporal good?" Luther says that people in the latter category "do the works of the law according to the letter without the spirit, i.e., for fear of punishment and not out of love for righteousness. According to their real intention, they would like to act differently if they could do so without being punished, although their will would become guilty. What do works that are done outwardly profit a man if his will is sinful before God, though humanly speaking his actions may appear righteous?"

B. The GRACE-minded person, on the other hand, loves the law and obeys it because it is the will of the God he loves. He delights in God's law (see Psalms 1:2; 112:1; 119:97). He really wants to obey it, even though he is weak and sometimes fails. Despite outward disobedience, he has an inward desire to obey (like Paul in Romans 7:22).

C. By way of contrast, the one hates punishment, and the other hates sin. The one loves the gift, and the other loves the giver. The one says "got to" obey; the other says "get to" obey. What about you? Do you try to obey only because you feel you HAVE to? Only because it is the *law*, and the law just HAS to be obeyed, even though you would rather not? Or do you obey freely because you want to please God? (Here is a hypothetical test question: If you suddenly discovered there were no heaven and no hell, would you still obey God's law? Or would you rejoice because now there is *no more reason* for you to obey it?)

III. What is your estimate of your own DEEDS or WORKS?
What is their value or function?

A. The LAW-minded one considers his deeds as a way of either earning or forfeiting his salvation. The GRACE-minded one sees his good deeds as loving expressions of thanksgiving for the gift of salvation, and his sins as wounds in the heart of God.

B. The LAW-mind sees his good works as SIN-offerings. He thinks that if he works hard enough, he can *make up for* his sins, like a balance scale where the good works equal or outweigh the bad. The GRACE-mind, though, sees his good works as THANK-offerings. He knows that salvation is a gift and that he cannot pay for it. He knows that if it really is a gift, all he can do is say "Thank you, God"—with his life.

C. The LAW-mind asks, "Have I done enough good works to be saved?' The GRACE-mind asks, "Am I trusting only in Jesus' works for my salvation? Have I done enough good works to please my Savior?"

D. The LAW-mind feels his salvation *depends* on how well he keeps the law. Every time he sins against God's law, he feels his salvation has been placed in jeopardy or forfeited. The GRACE-mind acknowledges his sin but knows that Christ has paid the debt of punishment owed for that sin.

E. The LAW-mind says, "I work in order to be saved." The GRACE-mind says, "I work because I have been saved." See Ephesians 2:8-10.

F. The LAW-mind feels that by keeping the ten commandments, or the sermon on the mount, or the golden rule, he is OK. He actually thinks that DOING these things makes him *good enough* to go to heaven. Or more commonly, he thinks that by NOT doing these things, he makes himself *too bad* to go to heaven. (These are two sides of the same coin of works-salvation.) But the GRACE-mind realizes that obedience and disobedience to law commands are not the *deciding* factors for determining his eternal destiny.

IV. What is your whole approach to SALVATION?

A. The LAW-mind seeks God by works; the GRACE-mind seeks God by faith.

B. The LAW-mind trusts his own personal ability to keep commandments; the GRACE-mind trusts God's ability to keep his promises.

C. One says DO; the other says DONE.

D. One says ACHIEVE; the other says BELIEVE.

E. One pleads MERIT; the other pleads MERCY.

F. One says ATTAINMENT; the other says ATONEMENT.

G. One pleads what WE have done; the other pleads what CHRIST has done.

H. One rests on his OWN righteousness; the other rests on GOD'S righteousness.

I. One rests assurance on personal obedience; the other rests assurance on God's love.

V. What is your estimate of GOD HIMSELF?

A. Is God gracious or not? Will He keep His promises or not? God wants to justify freely by His grace, and our response is to believe that He really means this! Dare we "let God be God"? Dare we believe His promises?

B. God is not an accountant who enjoys keeping record-books on us. He does not stand with eraser poised, eager for the chance to erase our names from the Book of Life. Let us not force Him into this mold. He wants to be a gracious God! He wants to mark your book "paid in full" and throw away the pencil and eraser!

C. God wants to be a GIVER, not a PAYMASTER. How would you feel if you gave someone you love a nice gift, and that person insisted on paying you for it? This is exactly what we are doing when we think that our works are somehow earning our salvation, when we think that our salvation depends on what we do day by day, as if our good works are earning our salvation and our sins are forfeiting it.

D. This exhortation is directed to earnest, sincere Christians who DO believe in God but who still are anxious about whether or not their salvation is in danger because they cannot do enough. My question to you is this: WILL YOU LET GOD BE GOD? Will you let him GIVE you your salvation? Will you let him write "paid in full" on your book? Where is your faith? Do you trust whole-heartedly in the blood of Jesus Christ? Do you really believe He has paid the penalty for your sins? Why do you still worry about going to hell?

Go ahead and DO YOUR VERY BEST—not to pay Him back, not to keep the credits ahead of the debits in a record book, not to see if your works can balance the gift—but in loving gratitude, and just because GOD IS GOD! Let God be gracious! Let him keep His promises!

CONCLUSION

The sum of the matter is this: is your life SELF-centered or GOD-centered?

A. Do you seek to obey the law for your own sake, for your own advantage; or do you do it for the glory of God? Do you love the gift more than the giver? Are you a greedy hireling who does what he is told so he can collect his pay, or a sullen slave who obeys to escape the whip? Or is your trust so fully resting in God that you put these thoughts aside and concentrate on obeying God because He is God, fully confident that He is and will be gracious?

B. The LAW-mind turns the spotlight on the self; the GRACE-mind turns it on God.

C. Remember that no one in this life will attain the ideal; no one will express the grace mentality perfectly. We will always have a tendency to think in terms of law, but we must fight against it and struggle to attain the GRACE-mind. We as Christians are somewhere between the two ends of the spectrum, but we are moving further from the one and closer to the other. In this lifetime it will never be a simple either/or, but rather a matter of less-and-more. With God's help, may we have less and less of the LAW-mind, and more and more of the GRACE-mind.

THE TEN COMMANDMENTS OF GRACE

This first appeared as a follow-up to an earlier website note, "Grace, Law, and the New Covenant." In my teaching about grace I make it quite clear that I believe traditional Restoration Movement thought comes up quite short on the subject of grace in many ways. Certain concepts that are deeply rooted in Restoration tradition are in fact significant barriers to a right understanding of grace. I have tried to sum them up very briefly in this list that I call "The Ten Commandments of Grace." All of these points are explained more fully in my book, *Set Free! What the Bible Says About Grace* (College Press, 2009). This list is on page 115 of that book. It has been pointed out that there is considerable irony in the way law and grace are combined in the very concept of this piece, as well as in its title.

ONE. Thou shalt not limit "law" in the crucial phrase "works of law" (Romans 3:20, 28; Galatians 2:16) to the Law of Moses, as if the point of grace is that we are justified by obedience to NEW Testament commandments rather than obedience to OLD Testament commandments.

TWO. Thou shalt not identify the "law" with which grace is contrasted (especially in Romans 6:14) as a law CODE (a list of commandments to live by, especially the Law of Moses) rather than as the law SYSTEM (attempting to be saved by obedience to one's law code).

THREE. Thou shalt present the "plan of salvation" as GRACE rather than as LAW (i.e., rather than as a law code by which we are saved). In the latter case it is a "plan of slavation," not a plan of salvation.

FOUR. Thou shalt distinguish between *works of law* (Romans 3:28) and *obedience to the gospel* (Romans 10:16; 2 Thessalonians 1:8) – both of which are "works" in the generic sense of "something you do." And, thou shalt explain that baptism is not only a work of GOD, but also a work of MAN in the latter sense (obedience to the gospel) – as is faith itself (John 6:26-29).

FIVE. Thou shalt not substitute Galatianism for grace, i.e., thou shalt not represent the sinner as being initially saved by grace, but kept saved by works.

SIX. Thou shalt neither teach nor imply that salvation is based on one's personal righteousness rather than on the righteousness of God in Christ.

SEVEN. Thou shalt not reject the validity of assurance of salvation, nor equate it with the false "once save, always saved" doctrine.

EIGHT. Thou shalt distinguish between the two parts of the "double cure": (1) justification or forgiveness, to take away sin's GUILT; and (2) regeneration/sanctification, to take away sin itself.

NINE. Thou shalt not represent baptism as being for the remission of PAST sins only.

TEN. Thou shalt not assume (because of a faulty understanding of 1 John 1:9) that every personal sin separates a Christian from the grace of God, and that the thus-fallen Christian remains in an unsaved, unforgiven state until he confesses the sin and prays for forgiveness.

GRACE AND THE COVENANTS

QUESTION: What is the connection between the New Covenant and the "grace system," to which you refer in your book, *Set Free! What the Bible Says About Grace* (pp. 50-51)? I have been taught by Restoration Movement teachers that grace is a New Covenant reality, i.e., that the New Covenant has replaced the Old Covenant with its legal requirements, and that we are now saved under the New Covenant by grace. In other words, to be under the New Covenant is synonymous with being saved by grace; the New Covenant and the "grace system" in some sense are identical. But you seem to be saying that the New Covenant is a law code and not soteric. How can this be? Because the New Covenant contains information about Jesus, sin, and salvation, I find it intellectually difficult NOT to equate the New Covenant with the grace system, and to assign some "soteric" value to the New Covenant. Can you clarify this issue for me?

ANSWER: My friend, there is quite a bit of confusion here, but I will TRY to clarify the matter! First, let's divide history into the pre-Christian and the Christian eras. The Christian era began, generally speaking, at Pentecost; that is when the New Covenant [NC] replaced the Old Covenant [OC] in its application. Everything before Pentecost is pre-Christian. (The fifty days between the resurrection and Pentecost are a kind of "neutral zone.") Then, let's divide the pre-Christian era into the pre-Mosaic and the Mosaic eras. In the time before Moses, God dealt with individuals on an *ad hoc* basis (e.g., Adam and Eve, Noah, Abraham). In the time from Moses to Christ's redemptive work (death, resurrection, ascension, enthronement, outpouring of the Holy Spirit), the Old Covenant was in force.

The OC is the formal arrangement through which God related to and by which he governed his chosen people, the Jews, during the Mosaic era. The NC is the formal arrangement through which God relates to and by which he governs or administers his chosen people, the church, during this Christian era. The instrument by which God exercised this government in the OC era was the canonical Old Testament Scriptures [OT], as they accumulated between Moses and Malachi. The instrument by which God exercises his government in the NC era is the canonical New Testament [NT]. DO NOT equate the Old COVENANT with the Old Testament SCRIPTURES. The OT contains the OC, but also much more. Likewise the New COVENANT must not be equated with the New Testament SCRIPTURES, since it is also much more. Yes, the NT Scriptures contain information about Jesus, sin, and salvation; but so did the OT Scriptures (with Jesus being referenced in prophecy)!

Now, how does all this relate to LAW and GRACE? First, when Paul (especially in Romans) refers to "law," sometimes he means a law CODE or list of commandments which God the Creator requires His creatures to obey, totally apart from any issues of salvation. Some of these commandments apply to all people in all ages; they are called "the moral law." Some are unique to the OC, and are the elements of the Law of Moses that applied only to the Jews under that covenant arrangement. Others are unique to the NC era. Thus the Jews were under the Mosaic Law Code, or the Old Covenant Law Code (the moral law plus their unique commandments); we today are under the New Covenant Law Code (the moral law plus our unique commandments). When the NC replaced the OC, the NC Law Code replaced the OC Law Code. This is the sense in which the OC and the Law of Moses (as a Law Code) have been abrogated or set aside.

But sometimes when Paul refers to "law," he means something quite different from a law code as such. He means instead the law as a SYSTEM OF SALVATION, in contrast with GRACE as a system of salvation. He means this especially in Romans 6:14-15, when he says that "you are not under law but under grace." Here "law" does NOT refer to ANY law code as such, including the Mosaic Law Code. Here Paul is saying that we are not under law AS A WAY OF SALVATION; rather, we are under grace AS A WAY OF SALVATION. To be under the law system of salvation is to be in a situation where you are counting on your obedience to your law code to make you right with God. The law system (which is quite valid) says you can be right with God by complete obedience to the law code that applies to you (the Mosaic Law Code, if you are a Jew living under the OC; or the NC Law Code, if you are living in this NC era). The problem is that this is only a theoretical possibility, since Paul's whole point is that NO ONE HAS complete obedience to his law code (Romans 3:9-20, 23), therefore no one can actually be right with God based on this system of salvation. The difference between law code and law system may be understood thus: everyone is under a law code (even those who are saved by grace); but only some of these are also under the law system (attempting to gain heaven by how well they obey their law code) and are therefore doomed to hell, since the law system cannot save sinners.

The gospel message is that God has provided another way or system of salvation, namely, GRACE. This system of salvation says that we are justified by faith in God's promises, not by how well we obey our law code (Romans 3:28). Everyone saved by grace still has a law code to obey; but obedience to this law code is not how we BECOME saved, nor is it how we STAY saved. "You are not under law" does NOT mean "You are not under a law code"; it means "You are not under law as a way of salvation." Grace as a way of salvation does NOT replace ANY law CODES; it is simply God's wonderful alternative to trying to be SAVED by obedience to one's law code. Salvation by grace comes only through Jesus's redemptive death on the cross; God offers sinners forgiveness of sins (justification) based on that substitutionary death.

Now here is the crucial point: this choice between two ways of salvation—the law system or the grace system—has NOTHING to do with any of the historical or covenantal divisions outlined above! These two salvation systems transcend the historical and covenant distinctions. These two salvation systems—law and grace—existed side by side from the moment sin began in the Garden of Eden. They constitute the only two ways a person may be "right with God," or enter heaven. The choice between them was available to Adam and Eve, to Abraham, and to the children of Israel; this choice is still available to us living today. The tragic fact, though, is that because of the universality of sin, no one can and will in fact be saved by the law system. Anyone who has ever been saved and who ever will be saved, will be saved by the grace system. Abraham was saved by grace. Moses was saved by grace. Elijah was saved by grace. John the Baptist was saved by grace (etc.). Grace did not begin with the NC; it was being freely bestowed throughout the pre-Christian era to all who accepted God's offer of forgiveness in faith and repentance. Though Jesus had not yet died, His redemptive death was a foreknown and predetermined event (Acts 2:23); and God was already dispensing its results before the fact (Romans 3:25).

I hope I have explained as succinctly as possible that there is NO sense in which grace as the only way of salvation for sinners can be equated with or limited to the New Covenant or the NC era.

ADDENDUM

I am attaching this Q&A to the above, because it also deals with a problem view of how the grace system is related to the covenants.

QUESTION: In a Bible study, a member asked me about (I can't recall the exact names, but I believe she said) 'star, morning and evening' dispensations. I don't recall the exact terms. A previous minister had taught on these dispensations. I know he is a Premillennial Dispensationalist. Is this part of dispensational theology, or am I confusing it with something else?

ANSWER: I do not know when it originated, but this view has been present in the Restoration Movement for many decades. In this view the three "dispensations" are called starlight, moonlight, and sunlight. In the Christian Church context, the one place I have seen it is in a very widely used study booklet from Standard Publishing called *Training for Service: A Survey of the Bible*, Student Handbook, by Orrin Root (rev. Eleanor Daniel, 1983). It is from lesson 6, "Three Dispensations." (I think this is something quite different from Dispensational Premillennialism.)

In this lesson a dispensation is described as the way "by which God dispenses or gives out His revelation, His blessing, and His punishment." It is alleged that God has done this over three periods of time, thus dealing with mankind "under three dispensations: Patriarchal, Jewish or Mosaic, and Christian." The terminology is applied thus: the Patriarchal age was the starlight dispensation, the age of promise. This was followed by the Mosaic or Jewish era, which was the moonlight dispensation, or dispensation of law. Under this dispensation God blessed His people when they obeyed, and punished them when they disobeyed. Jesus then brought the new and present sunlight dispensation, with His death opening the way for the forgiveness of sins. "God now dispenses or gives salvation and blessing by His grace, not because we deserve them." This is the *Christian* dispensation, and "is called the *dispensation of grace* because Christians rely on God's grace for their salvation" (Root, *Training for Service*, pp. 32-33).

In my course on grace I use this as an example of one of the FALSE ideas of grace that permeate the Restoration Movement, i.e., that the distinction between law and grace is a matter of historical sequence, with salvation by law applying to the Old Covenant era and salvation by grace applying only to the New Covenant era. This is totally false. The law system of relating to God and the grace system as an alternative of relating to God have both been present side by side ever since sin entered the world in the Garden of Eden. They are *not sequential.* These two ways of relating to God—i.e., law or grace—have NOTHING to do with the distinction between the Old and New Covenants, nor with the distinction between the Old Testament Scriptures and the New Testament Scriptures. It is true that the New Testament revelation gives the fuller *explanation* of how this all works, but God has been *applying* grace for salvation ever since Adam and Eve.

I cannot emphasize strongly enough just how WRONG this "three-dispensations" idea is, and how critical a hindrance it is to a right understanding of grace. (I deal with this view briefly in my book, *Set Free: What the Bible Says About Grace*, pp. 111-112.)

WESLEYAN GRACE

QUESTION: The Wesleyan church believes there are two forms of grace. I don't understand this. Their doctrine is similar to the Christian Church. Can you help me understand this?

ANSWER: Wesleyanism includes those groups and denominations that have grown out of the teachings of John Wesley (1703-1791). These include Methodist churches, Holiness churches, and many Pentecostal churches. The theological content of these groups is similar to the Christian Church (Restoration Movement) in one main way: it is non-Calvinist, or Arminian; it accepts a measure of truly free will in human beings. In many other ways it is very different from the Christian Church.

The main way Wesleyanism differs from most other Protestant groups is in its view of the two works of grace. This should not be confused with what is called the "double cure" of grace, a term I took over from the song "Rock of Ages" and a concept that is widely recognized in Christendom. This "double cure" is the distinction between two aspects of salvation: (1) God saves us from the legal consequences of sin—guilt and condemnation—by *justifying* or forgiving us on the basis of the substitutionary atonement of Jesus. (2) God cures the sinfulness that has corrupted our hearts by *regenerating* and *sanctifying* us by the healing work of the indwelling Holy Spirit. Wesleyanism accepts both of these aspects of salvation, but this is not what they mean by "the two works of grace."

As a matter of terminology, the question above refers to the Wesleyan belief in two "forms" of grace. I am assuming that this is referring to what is more often called the two "works" of grace, since we commonly hear about what Wesleyans call "the second work of grace." This is definitely a distinctive Wesleyan belief.

In Wesleyan theology the FIRST work of grace is the initial gift of salvation, which is seen as including the "double cure" mentioned above: (1) justification and (2) usually regeneration or the new birth. This first work is the conversion event, the moment when the person becomes saved. It happens when the sinner chooses to believe and repent, and in the Zwinglian tradition this is not necessarily associated with water baptism (which will probably happen later as a church ceremony). At this salvation moment the person begins to live under the grace of God, and begins to pursue sanctification. All of this is the result of the *first* work of grace.

However, something is still lacking. That which is lacking has to do not with justification, but with sanctification. There is an initial sanctification bestowed at conversion, and the believer proceeds to grow in grace and knowledge. But according to Wesleyanism, God has a great deal more in store for the convert. This "something more" is the SECOND work of grace.

This second work of grace is something that used to be pursued by Wesleyans (and still is by some) with the fervor and expectation of sinners seeking salvation itself. It was/is something to be prayed for at the mercy seat, but the seeker himself or herself has no control over when and how it might be bestowed. When God decides the time is right, it will happen. It is seen as a second out-pouring of the Holy Spirit, interpreted as the Biblical "baptism in the Holy Spirit." The purpose and result of this out-pouring is seen as full sanctification or entire sanctification, and some interpret this as the ability to live above sin from that moment on. This is a kind of perfectionism. It is emphasized mainly in the Holiness churches. In Pentecostalism this baptism of the Holy Spirit became associated not just with holiness but especially with miraculous gifts such as tongue-speaking.

Basically, there is no Biblical basis for such a "second" work of grace, a point that has been well established by Frederick Dale Bruner in his book, *A Theology of the Holy Spirit* (Eerdmans 1970). Bruner shows very clearly that there is no true Biblical basis for such a second work of the Holy Spirit. I recommend his book for those who want to study this in detail.

I have a brief discussion of this view in my large book on the Holy Spirit, *Power from on High: What the Bible Says About the Holy Spirit* (College Press, 2007). See the index entry, "second work of grace."

My view is that what we should be emphasizing is the *double cure* of grace, which is received at conversion, after faith and repentance and specifically *during water baptism*. Contrary to the Wesleyan view, which separates water baptism from Spirit baptism, the Bible teaches that there is only ONE baptism in Christian experience (Ephesians 4:5), which includes at the same time both baptism in water and baptism in the Holy Spirit (1 Corinthians 12:13) in one event. The fact that Paul says with apostolic authority that there is only *one baptism* is usually ignored by most of Christendom. Though we disagree as to when it occurs, we can agree with Wesleyanism that our conversion experience is the "first work of grace."

From this point on the believer is completely justified, and continues to become more and more holy (sanctified) as God is holy (1 Peter 1:15-16), throughout his or her Christian life. Contrary to Wesleyan theology, there is no "second" crisis experience *in this life* resulting in a significant bump-up to complete holiness. Based on my study of Romans 6-8, I have concluded that complete sanctification will not be possible until our spirits are separated from our bodies at death. This is because the "first work of grace," i.e., our reception of the double cure in baptism, regenerated only our spirits (Romans 6:6) and did not cleanse our bodies from their sinfulness. Through the power of our regenerated spirits (Romans 6:1-14) and of the indwelling Holy Spirit (Romans 8:1ff.), we can suppress but not eliminate these sinful urges of the body in this lifetime. After death, though, the "second work of grace" can be accomplished because then our bodiless spirits are "made perfect" in a moral sense (Hebrews 12:23)—bestowing complete sanctification. Then at the second coming we will be made completely, humanly perfect when our sanctified spirit will be rejoined with a redeemed, glorified body (Romans 8:23; Philippians 3:21). This will be our full glorification, which we can call the "third work of grace"! We will then be ready for eternal life in the new heavens and new earth.

PLAN OF SALVATION—OR PLAN OF SLAVATION?

Over the decades there have been many versions of the Restoration Movement's so-called "five-finger exercise," also called the "plan of salvation." Most of us are probably familiar with Walter Scott's pioneering synergistic version of it, based on Acts 2:38: (1) believe, (2) repent, and (3) be baptized; and you will receive (4) forgiveness of sins and the (5) gift of the Holy Spirit.

The one that was most common in the Restoration circles I grew up in, however, went like this: (1) believe, (2) repent, (3) confess, (4) be baptized, and (5) live the Christian life—and you will be saved. I did not realize it then, but there came a time when I wished we had stuck with Scott's original version. This was after I had developed a better understanding of the Biblical doctrine of the grace of God, especially regarding the difference between law and grace. The more I learned about Romans 3:28, and the difference between justification by faith and justification by works of law; and about Romans 6:14, and the difference between the law system of salvation and the grace system, the more I realized that the five-finger exercise as I knew it was more a plan of *slavation* than a plan of *salvation.*

I don't know exactly when, but I came to see that this way of explaining "how to be saved" is basically salvation by works (by law-keeping) rather than salvation by grace. Specifically, it is a law system of salvation known as Galatianism. It gets it name from the false teaching the Apostle Paul is attacking and refuting in his letter to the Galatians, i.e., the teaching of the Judaizers. In essence, they were teaching that one *becomes* saved by accepting Jesus as Savior, and then *stays* saved by submitting to the law of Moses. Along the way the name Galatianism has been applied to any view that says one becomes saved by faith and stays saved by works. It is not surprising that the Restoration Movement gravitated into this way of thinking, since it was specifically taught by Alexander Campbell.[1] In the five-step exercise explained above, the first four do explain how to *become* saved by grace, but the fifth step ("live the holy life") is basically saying that we *stay* saved by law-keeping.

Thus I have concluded that this way of explaining the five-finger exercise over the years has been representing salvation as just another law system rather than as a gift of God's grace. Several decades ago, I was asked to speak on the subject of "the plan of salvation" at a regional church gathering. As I was trying to type out my message, I kept making the same typographical error over and over. Almost every time I tried to type "plan of salvation," it unintentionally came out as "plan of *slavation*." All at once it dawned on me: the Galatianist version of the five-finger exercise is just that—a "plan of *slavation*"! By presenting these five points as a series of stair-steps the sinner must climb to reach salvation (with the last one being a doozy!), we have been enslaving converts to the law mentality from the very beginning of their Christian lives.

Some years ago I was interested to see that Dr. David Eubanks (from what was then Johnson Bible College) had sensed the need to revise the "plan" somewhat. He suggested a "four-finger exercise," in which the whole hand is compared with faith and the four fingers represent repentance, confession, baptism, and Christian living as growing out of faith just as the four fingers extend out from the palm. He explained that this "helps to place obedience in its proper perspective to faith, to keep us clear of relegating faith to merely a step in the plan of salvation, to prevent any false conflict between the Biblical doctrine of justification by faith and the necessity of obedience, and to head off false charges that we teach water regeneration and justification by works."[2]

Bravo! I applaud Brother Eubanks' readiness to break with tradition when that is necessary to make our doctrine more Biblical, and I consider this suggestion to be a step in the right direction toward a proper understanding of the faith-and-works issue. It does indeed show the unique relation between faith and salvation. The suggestion does not go far enough, however, since it still leaves the impression that repentance, confession, baptism, and Christian living (i.e., good works) have the same kind of necessity when related to salvation. Leaving Christian living as somehow equivalent to repentance, confession, and baptism will either diminish the meaning of baptism or elevate Christian living to the necessity of means, thus taking us back into a works-salvation stance.

Perhaps we will just have to abandon the use of the hand and its fingers as a "handy" way of illustrating the "plan of salvation"!

I have been suggesting for quite some time[3] that we consider using a different kind of formula for showing the unsaved how to receive salvation and for leading them through the conversion experience. It is not intended to be comprehensive since it does not specifically mention all the conditions for receiving salvation, but it does broaden the scope to include God's part in the process. It also has the benefit of using phrases that are directly taken from two brief synoptic sections of the Word of God: Ephesians 2:8-10 and Colossians 2:12. In these parallel verses Paul says: "For **by grace** you have been saved **through faith**; and that not of yourselves, it is the gift of God; not as a result of works, that no one should boast. For we are His workmanship, created in Christ Jesus **for good works**, which God prepared beforehand that we should walk in them" (Ephesians 2:8-10). And, "Having been buried with him **in baptism**, in which you were also raised up with Him **through faith** in the working of God, who raised Him from the dead" (Colossians 2:12).

My suggestion is that we teach sinners that they are saved *by* grace, *through* faith, *in* baptism, *for* good works. In this formula the preposition "by" in the phrase "by grace" identifies grace, specifically the redemptive work of Jesus Christ, as the BASIS of salvation. This helps to keep the spotlight where it belongs. It is very important that a sinner understand the grace-character of salvation from the very beginning, so that the succeeding steps will not be misconstrued as in any way earning or deserving God's gifts.

The preposition "through" in the phrase "through faith" shows the MEANS by which we sinners receive the double cure of grace: we appropriate it through faith in Jesus. This is the proper application of the *sola fidei* concept. Some may wonder how something so frail as faith can have such power. But the power is not in the faith itself; it lies rather in the object of faith: the redemptive death and resurrection of our Lord and Savior.

This formula itself does not mention repentance and confession, but this is where these conditions should be included in a presentation to sinners. Faith as the proper attitude toward God will always be accompanied by repentance as the proper attitude toward sin. Taking God at his word (which is the essence of faith as such) will involve a hatred of sin and a deep desire to be rid of it in our lives. Confession likewise is a natural concomitant of faith, since it is specifically a confession of one's faith in Jesus and his saving work. (See Romans 10:9-10.)

The third element of the formula is "in baptism," which identifies the occasion (time and place) when God has promised to give the double cure. This phrase is specifically used by Paul in Colossians 2:12, which is parallel in content with Ephesians 2:8-10, whence come the other phrases in the formula. A common objection is that the baptism in Colossians 2:12 must be a reference to *spiritual* baptism only, since it is unequivocally described as the time of salvation and since (so it is alleged) it is not possible for water baptism—a "work"—to be so related to salvation. This objection has been dealt with in other places, but I will point out here that this interpretation of the baptism in Colossians 2:12 puts most Protestants in conflict with the Apostle Paul. This is so because it creates a situation in which Christians actually experience *two* baptisms: the spiritual baptism which brings salvation, and water baptism as a subsequent testimony to it. Paul, however, emphatically says in Ephesians 4:5 that there is only *one* baptism, which is at the *same time* a baptism in water and in the Holy Spirit.

The last item in the formula, "for good works," shows how post-baptismal "living the Christian life" fits into the picture. We are not saved *by* such works, as Paul specifically says in Ephesians 2:9. Rather, we are saved *for* such works, as verse 10 says. They are the *result* of God's saving workmanship, namely, the Holy Spirit's work of *new creation* (regeneration, new birth, resurrection) which he performed upon us in the moment of baptism. Certainly it is necessary for us to do good works; but such holy living has the necessity of *precept*, not the necessity of *means*.

I conclude that the best approach to the question of how faith and works are related to salvation is summed up thus: we are saved by grace, through faith, in baptism, for good works.

ENDNOTES

[1] See my discussion of this in my book, *Set Free! What the Bible Says About Grace* (College Press, 2009), pp. 274-276. This brief essay is actually an updated version of pp. 241-244 in that book.

[2] David L. Eubanks, "The Four-Finger Exercise," *Blue and White*, July-August 1978.

[3] See my little book, *His Truth*, first published by Standard Publishing in Cincinnati in 1980, chapter 10, "Truth About Conversion: Man's Response." It is now published by Wipf and Stock Publishers in Eugene, OR.

PART FOUR

JUSTIFICATION

THE HEART OF THE GOSPEL: ROMANS 3:21-26

Romans is my favorite book of the Bible, and Romans 3:21-26 is my favorite passage in this epistle. This lesson is about that passage; hence, this is my favorite Bible lesson! (It can be found in outline form on pp. 190-193 in my book, *Set Free! What the Bible Says About Grace* [College Press, 2009].)

The first main section of Romans (1:18-3:20) is all about LAW. It makes three points: (1) Everyone knows some law. (2) Everyone has broken this law at some point. (3) Thus no one can be right with God (i.e., justified) by law-keeping. As Paul says at the end of this section, by works of law (i.e., by how well one is able to keep the law commands for which he is responsible), no flesh will be justified.

What, then, is our hope for eternal life? This is what Paul explains in the next main section (3:21-5:21), beginning with 3:21-26. This is the paragraph we are examining here. In it Paul explains HOW SINNERS CAN BE RIGHT WITH GOD'S LAW.

Paul's teaching in this paragraph conjures up the image of a courtroom, with a defendant, his lawyer, a judge, and a jury (think of Perry Mason, Matlock, Law and Order, or John Grisham). In a fictional courtroom, *usually* (though not always) the innocent are cleared and the guilty are exposed. In this Biblical courtroom scene, however, there are no innocents (Romans 3:10). We are all defendants charged with a crime, we are all on trial before God, and we all are actually guilty as charged. This is the context in which Paul explains the crucial doctrine of JUSTIFICATION. The question is: How will the Judge decide in our case?

I. THE CRIME: The Sinner's "Problem with the Law" (v. 23).

Romans 3:23 sums up the problem: "All have sinned." (This was one of the main points in 1:18-3:20, as Paul concluded in 3:9, "We have already charged that both Jews and Greeks are all under sin.") We should remember that the Bible describes sin as law-breaking: "Everyone who practices sin also practices lawlessness; and sin is lawlessness" (1 John 3:4). The Greek word is *anomia*, which combines the word for law (*nomos*) with the negating alpha (*a-*). It thus means "opposition to the law, contrary to the law." This *anomia* takes two forms. It is first a state of the heart, an ATTITUDE of rebellion against and disrespect for the law. This is the concept of lawlessness. Also, it is the ACT of breaking the law. Thus some versions translate it "the transgression of the law" (KJV) or "the breaking of law" (Holman's CSB).

Paul completes the thought of verse 23 with these words: "And fall short of the glory of God." This verb is present tense; it refers to the *state* in which we exist as a consequence of sin. The Greek word is *hystereō*, which means "to lack, be deficient in, be wanting, fall behind." It suggests "being weighed in the balances, and found wanting" (Daniel 5:27). We don't measure up—to the glory of God.

"The glory of God" refers to the glory of God's holiness that is supposed to be shining forth from our lives by virtue of our being made in His image (Matthew 5:16, 48; 1 Peter 1:15-16). Every aspect of our lives should glorify God (1 Corinthians 10:31). However, because of our sinfulness (lawlessness!), we do not show forth that glory of God as we are supposed to do and are obligated to do. We are like faulty 3-way, 100-watt light bulbs that will shine at only 33 or 50 watts—or not at all.

Thus, as sinners, we are "in trouble with the law." We have a *legal* problem. We stand *guilty* before God the Judge (Romans 3:19; James 2:10). In the terminology of legal dramas, each of us is what is called "the perp" (the perpetrator of the crime). This guilt is an objective state in connection with the law, and should not be confused with subjective guilt *feelings*.

Our situation thus seems to be hopeless. We are facing the maximum penalty, which is like a debt we owe to God, namely, the debt of eternal punishment in hell. See Matthew 6:12; Luke 13:4; Matthew 18:23-25. Also, the evidence against us is overwhelming, and it cannot be hidden from the omniscient God, who is our Judge. And as our Judge, He is very strict and fair.

As they used to say on the original TV drama *Hawaii 5-0*, "Book 'em, Danno!"

II. THE POSSIBILITY OF ACQUITTAL.

The point of this paragraph in Romans (3:21-26) is this: It IS possible for sinners to be "right with the law" again! Our hope and our goal are to "beat the rap." But in fictional stories, usually only the innocent go free, and the guilty get what's coming to them. But we are guilty! How can we hope to "get off"?

Being right with the law means being in a state of *righteousness*. ("Righteousness" basically means "satisfying the requirements of the law.") So if we are judged strictly by the rules of law, the only way to be acquitted is to be innocent. But we are guilty! And yet we seek acquittal—or at least we seek to escape the punishment we deserve! Is there any way this can happen? Is there some way we can make up for our sins, or avoid the due consequences of our sins?

As sinners, and according to the provisions of law, the ONLY way we can be in a state of righteousness—i.e., the only way we can personally satisfy the requirements of the law—is to suffer the full *penalty* deserved by our sins (i.e., eternity in hell). Is our case hopeless, then?

NO! There is another *kind* of righteousness, another *way* for even *a sinner* to be right with the law, a way that is different from anything the law can provide. It is "outside the law," or "apart from law" (v. 21). It has been revealed or made known through the *gospel* of Jesus Christ (1:17), specifically in the event of the cross. "Apart from law" (v. 21) means "apart from the law SYSTEM." The law system (i.e., how law works) CANNOT bring sinners into a state of righteousness except by applying the penalty, i.e., by condemning us to hell forever. But we are talking now about the GRACE system, and the grace system is different! The grace system allows us to be right with the law without having to suffer its penalty, even though we have sinned!

In other words, even though we have sinned, the Judge can still JUSTIFY us (v. 24). He is the One who "justifies the ungodly" (4:5)! To be "justified" means having the Judge say "No penalty for you!" or "I declare you to be right with the law, just as you are!" "To justify" is a legal term; it is the opposite of "to condemn." (See Deuteronomy 25:1; Proverbs 17:15; Romans 8:33-34.) "To be justified" means the Judge *declares* us righteous; He does not *make* us righteous. This meaning of "justify" is seen in Luke 7:29, which literally says that people "justified God," i.e., *declared* Him to be a righteous God.

III. THE LAWYER. The only way we guilty law-breakers can be justified is to *have the right lawyer* (which, of course, is every criminal's dream)!

When you are in trouble with the law, you need a good lawyer, one who can "get you off" even though you are guilty. You need a lawyer who can say, "Don't worry! Leave everything to me. I will handle your case; I will take care of it. I will *make sure* you don't serve any time. And I am your only hope." In the divine courtroom, the only one who can do this is *Jesus* (vv. 22, 24), our *paraklētos*, or "defense advocate" (1 John 2:1).

The only way sinners can "beat the rap" of sin is to turn their case over completely to Jesus: "through faith in Jesus Christ" (v. 22). No matter how guilty you are, as your lawyer Jesus absolutely guarantees that you won't serve any time; i.e., he guarantees that the Judge will *justify* you!

IV. THE STRATEGY. How does Jesus accomplish this?

If you were actually on trial here in an earthly court, e.g., for murder, your lawyer would have to decide: how are we going to approach this case—especially if you are actually guilty? What strategy can "get you off"—or at least have the judge declare: "No penalty for you"? How would your lawyer accomplish this? By calling lots of character witnesses? By entering an insanity plea? Self-defense? Bribe the jury? Lie like a dog? Sometimes these things actually occur in earthly courts, but they won't work in the divine courtroom.

Nevertheless, Jesus, our defense attorney before the heavenly Judge, does have a strategy, a "gimmick" that He guarantees will be successful! This strategy, however, must be very different from anything the law system can provide—and it is! Jesus's defense plan is a sure-fire system of getting around the law, a way to "get us off"; but it works in a totally different way from the way law itself works. It is "apart from law" (v. 21a).

This strategy is called GRACE (v. 24). It is the "grace defense." Grace is a way of handling our legal problem, a way of getting the Judge to JUSTIFY us by declaring "No penalty for you!". How does Jesus, our defense lawyer, pull this off? *He pays off the Judge!* And He does it with His own resources! This is the "grace defense"! How does it work? (This is not as gross as it sounds!)

This payment is described as an act of *redemption* (v. 24), i.e., setting us free by paying a price. (See Exodus 13:11-13; Numbers 18:14-16; 1 Peter 1:18-19; Ephesians 1:7.) What is the redemption or ransom price? Jesus' own blood (His life), paid to God the Father (Matthew 20:28).

It is described also as an act of *propitiation*, or sacrifice of atonement (v. 25). "To propitiate" literally means "to turn aside wrath by means of an offering." Jesus becomes that offering, our *hilasmos*, our *hilastērion*: the "offering that turns away wrath." Propitiation is common in pagan religions. Pagans assume their gods are angry with them; thus they seek to provide their own offerings to turn away this wrath.

How is Christian propitiation different from this? Because in Christianity the true God Himself, by His gracious love, provides the only offering that is capable of turning away His own wrath: Jesus our propitiation (1 John 4:10; John 3:16). Jesus our lawyer accomplishes this propitiation *Himself*; His offering of Himself on the cross pays the full penalty for our sins. He is not only our defense advocate (1 John 2:1); He is also the very "offering that turns away wrath"—the propitiation itself (1 John 2:2).

This is his *strategy*—the strategy of grace, the "grace defense"—that keeps us from having to suffer the deserved penalty for our sins. It works every time!

"But can I *afford* such a lawyer? Won't He cost me a lot?" Yes and no. On the one hand, His services are FREE: *grace* is a GIFT (v. 24). But He requires that you *trust Him completely* to take care of your case (vv. 22, 25, "through faith in His blood"). On the other hand, it costs you EVERYTHING. You have to turn your whole life over to Him. There is no "cheap grace," to use Bonhoeffer's term.

V. THE JUDGE. What does the Judge Himself think about all of this? It was *His* idea (vv. 25-26)!

It was God the Judge Himself who set Jesus forth as the propitiation, or atoning sacrifice (v. 25a). He was already using the grace system even before Jesus went to the cross; He was forgiving "the sins previously committed," for those who believed, through all of history ever since Adam and Eve (v. 25b).

Redemption through the blood of Jesus is the only strategy that allows God to be true to both sides of His nature (v. 26). Under this system God is JUST, because the requirements of the law (for penalty) are satisfied—by Jesus. Thus His holy wrath is satisfied. But He is also then free to JUSTIFY anyone who takes on Jesus as his defense lawyer and trusts his eternity to the grace strategy. Thus His gracious love is satisfied.

CONCLUSION

This passage, Romans 3:21-26, is the heart and core not only of Romans but also of the whole Bible. Leon Morris (*The Epistle to the Romans*, 173) says it is "possibly the most important single paragraph ever written." He is correct.

THE RIGHTEOUSNESS OF GOD IN THE GOSPEL: ROMANS 1:16-17

QUESTION: In Romans 1:16-17 Paul says that the righteousness of God is revealed in the Gospel. The word "gospel" means "good news." In what sense can the righteousness of God be good news for sinners?

ANSWER: That God is righteous means that He must always be true to Himself; He must always be true to every aspect of His nature. This is His consistency of character. It means that He must be true BOTH to His holy nature (his perfect moral purity) AND to His loving nature.

In reference to the former, "righteousness" includes seeing that the requirements of His LAW are satisfied: *either* through obedience to its commands *or* through the suffering of its penalties. God would prefer that it be done through the former; but if it is not, His righteousness demands that His law's penalty must be applied.

Thus, God maintains the integrity of His law—i.e., He maintains His own righteousness—by requiring its commands to be obeyed, and by imposing the penalty of eternal suffering upon those who disobey. Sadly, sin is simply a fact. Therefore His holy wrath *must* be applied and satisfied, for His own righteousness' sake.

Here is where the question arises: in what sense can the reality of God's righteousness be *good news* to sinners? How can the righteousness of God be the subject of the GOSPEL message (Romans 1:16-17)?

We can answer this question through the following imagery. *every time* we sin, we are figuratively writing out an IOU to God: "I owe you, God, the debt of eternal punishment in hell." Here is where the righteousness of God comes in: because God is righteous, his righteousness demands that these debts—these IOUs—*must* be paid. How will this be accomplished? This can happen in two ways: either under the system of *law*, or under the system of *grace*.

Under the LAW system, God will uphold His righteousness (i.e., He will satisfy the requirements of His law) by calling in all of these IOUs on the day of judgment. On this day His righteousness will take the form of His holy wrath, which He will begin to pour out upon sinners *directly*, sentencing them to eternity in hell. In this way God is true to His holy nature. His justice is satisfied, in reference to His holiness.

But – there is *another* way that He can uphold His righteousness: a way motivated and devised by His LOVE (John 3:16; 1 John 4:9-10). This is the way of grace. Under the GRACE system, God also bestows His righteousness upon sinners, but in a very different way. I.e., He does so through the *gospel* (see Romans 1:17). Here the satisfaction of His law's requirement for penalty upon the disobedient is achieved through the substitutionary atonement of Jesus, the sin-bearer. How does this work? There are two steps.

First, the righteous Father pours out the requirements of His holy wrath directly upon *Jesus*. Jesus becomes the "designated sinner" who takes the place of all actual sinners. He is our substitute as He suffers within Himself the full force of sin's penalty. He suffers the equivalent of eternity in hell for the whole human race.

Remember: as sinners, we owe God the debt of eternal suffering in hell. But here is where Jesus comes into the picture. He takes upon Himself *all* the IOUs generated by all the sins of all the world, and carries them to the cross, and pays them in full: Colossians 2:13-15. See verse 14: God saved us "by canceling the record of debt that stood against us with its legal demands. This he set aside, nailing it to the cross" (ESV).

This is the correct understanding of Colossians 2:14. The Greek word for "record of debt" is *cheirographon*, literally, "handwriting." It has nothing to do with any law code (contra the NIV's "written code"), Mosaic or otherwise. It refers to a handwritten document, a certificate of indebtedness – like an IOU. According to Ceslas Spicq, *Theological Lexicon of the New Testament* (III:508-509), this word was often used in the papyri as "a technical term meaning 'acknowledgment of debt,' i.e., the receipt signed by a debtor, who acknowledges that he owes a certain sum and undertakes to repay it." "Once the invoice was paid or the note was honored, it was canceled with two crosswise strokes."

Commenting on this last statement ("canceled with two crosswise strokes"), Spicq cites a late first-century document that says, *ekeleuse to cheirographon chiasthenai* ("he ordered a cross to be marked on the invoice"). The word for "mark a cross on" is *chiazō*, which means "to shape like the letter *chi*" – which is the shape of an X (two lines crossing one another), i.e. , the shape of a cross. This reminds us of Colossians 2:14, which says God removed our *cheirographon* by "nailing it to the cross."

God's holy nature is thus righteously satisfied. God thus maintains His righteousness, His justice, in reference to His HOLINESS.

But now comes the second step. In the act of saving the *individual* sinner, in the moment of conversion, God gathers up all the *canceled IOUs* relating to that person's sins (past and future), wraps them up in a gift package, and presents them to him or her as a free gift. These canceled IOUs (the cancelation of our deserved eternal punishment in hell, canceled by means of the substitutionary atonement of Jesus) represent God's righteousness being bestowed upon us as God's gift of grace. See Romans 3:22; 10:3; Colossians 3:9.

In this way God's own righteousness—the satisfaction of the law's requirement of penalty for disobedience—is bestowed upon us *indirectly*, having been bestowed *directly* upon Jesus and having thus been satisfied by Jesus Christ in our place. We can think of this gift of God's righteousness as something like a *receipt* that says, "This sinner's eternal penalty for his/her sins has been paid in full by Jesus Christ. There is therefore now no condemnation awaiting this person, since he/she is now in union with Jesus Christ." See Romans 8:1.

The moment we receive this receipt, i.e., this certificate guaranteeing that the penalty for our sins has been paid, we are JUSTIFIED: the Judge says, "No penalty for you!" By justifying us *in this manner*, God maintains His righteousness (His "justice"), in reference to His *love*. And even though in His love He is justifying us, He is still just (i.e., righteous) in terms of His *holiness* (Romans 3:26). This is the essence of Romans 3:21-26, and it is the essence of the "good news" of the gospel.

RIGHTEOUSNESS: IMPUTED OR IMPARTED?

QUESTION: Can you explain the difference between "imputed righteousness" and "imparted righteousness"?

ANSWER: The distinction between imparted and imputed righteousness has to do with their relation to salvation, especially as this relates to the definition of justification. This is important because the Bible pictures sinners as being saved by "the righteousness of God" (Romans 1:17; 3:21-22; 2 Corinthians 5:21; Philippians 3:9). I.e., God saves us by transferring His own righteousness to us in some way—by imparting it, or imputing it, or both.

What is "righteousness" as such? Most fundamentally, righteousness means "conformity to a norm," i.e., to whatever norm is appropriate for that particular entity. Regarding human beings, the norm to which we are supposed to conform is God's law. To be "righteous" thus means to *satisfy the requirements of the law.* Here it is important to see that the law has two parts: commandments and penalties. Thus we as human beings can be righteous in one of two ways: we can satisfy the *commandments* of the law (= active righteousness), or we can satisfy the *penalty* of the law (= passive righteousness). Under the law system of relating to God, one can acquire heaven by the former through perfect obedience to all the applicable commandments of the law. But if we fail to conform to the law in even one of its commands (James 2:10), then the only way to be "right with the law" (i.e., righteous) is to satisfy its penalty, which is hell.

How is this related to "the righteousness of God"? Is there a norm to which God Himself must conform in order to be righteous? In fact, there is, and here is how it works: God is perfectly righteous because at all times His decisions and deeds are in perfect conformity with His *nature*. His own nature is the norm for His actions, and He never acts contrary to His nature. He is always faithful and true to Himself, which includes a complete faithfulness to His own WORD. Part of His Word is His law, including both its commandments and its warnings. God's perfect righteousness includes the fact that He will always uphold the integrity of the law He has applied to us as His creatures.

In other words, the RIGHTEOUS GOD will always make sure that the requirements of His law are satisfied. God's own righteousness is glorified when we, His creatures, satisfy the *commands* of His law by obeying them. But if we sin (i.e., disobey the law's commands), God's righteousness is still satisfied through the application of the law's *penalty* (hell) to us as lawbreakers. The problem for God is that ALL human beings are sinners (Romans 3:10, 23); thus to maintain His own righteousness He must condemn all of us to hell. But He does not want to do this; He created us human beings for the very purpose of having eternal fellowship with us. So He has a dilemma: how can He save at least some human beings from the righteous consequences of their sins, and at the same time maintain His own righteousness by upholding the integrity of His law?

The answer is that He transfers His own righteousness to us; and He does this in two ways. These two ways correspond to the two parts of the "double cure" of salvation: justification (on the one hand), and regeneration/sanctification (on the other). Here is where the terms *imparting* and *imputing* enter the picture. God *imparts* righteousness to us by giving us enabling grace, i.e., by giving us the moral power to obey the law's commands through His works of regeneration and sanctification.

When God's grace empowers us to live a holy life, this holiness is regarded as having been imparted to us by God because it is His power working within us that enables us to produce it (Philippians 2:13).

The imputation of righteousness is very different. God *imputes* righteousness to us by "doctoring the books," so to speak. As individuals we can think of our lives as being represented before God by a journal that details all of our deeds, both good and bad, and which keeps a running tally of our "account" in terms of what we owe to God. Once even one sin (James 2:10) is entered into this journal, it is recorded that we owe to God the penalty of eternity in hell because of our sin. No good deed that we do is able to counteract this debt, since we already owe to God every act of obedience that we can perform (Luke 17:10). Thus every time we sin, the debt of eternal punishment just gets more intense, with no relief in sight.

So how can any of us be saved? Imputed righteousness to the rescue! Jesus came and lived a perfect life so that He personally would not owe to the Father eternity in hell. This prepared Him to step into our shoes, and accept the penalty of eternal hell in our place, or pay the debt of eternal punishment for us. This is His work of propitiation, which is the heart of the substitutionary atonement (Romans 3:25). For those of us (any sinners) who trust God's promises and obey the gospel, God transfers Jesus's payment of the eternal penalty for sin to our account, thus canceling the sin-debt that we owe. This is the essence of imputation: the transfer of Jesus' satisfaction of the law's penalty (i.e., God's passive righteousness) to our journal-account, so that His righteousness is counted as our own. ("Imputation" is actually a bookkeeping term.)

This is the basis for the heart of the grace given to us in the moment of salvation, namely, our justification (which is equivalent to forgiveness of sins). Justification is the declaration of God, in His role as Judge, that we are considered righteous before Him, in the sense that He counts our penalty as having already been paid. "There is therefore now no condemnation to those who are in Christ Jesus" (Romans 8:1) – this is the essence of justification. To be justified is to have the Judge make this pronouncement over you: "NO PENALTY FOR YOU!" He does this solely on the basis of imputed righteousness.

Does this mean that imparted righteousness is irrelevant? Not at all! The key here is the distinction between the two parts of the double cure. It is true that *justification* is received ONLY on the basis of *imputed* righteousness (i.e., the blood of Christ). We are not justified by imparted righteousness (which is basically the same as our works). However, there is more to salvation than being justified (forgiven); there is also the change in our spiritual nature called regeneration (a one-time work of the Holy Spirit in baptism) and sanctification (the ongoing pursuit of holy living through the power of the indwelling Spirit). The Spirit's works of regeneration and sanctification are the essence of imparted righteousness.

WHAT JUSTIFIES US?

QUESTION: Are we justified by Christ's death, or by our faith in Christ?

ANSWER: Both are involved, but in different ways. Romans 5:9 says we are "justified by his blood," and Romans 3:28 says that "a man is justified by faith." Justification (equivalent to forgiveness of sins) is God's declaration that he accepts us as righteous before the law, in the sense that our debt of eternal punishment has been canceled. To be justified means that God, in his role as Judge, looks at us and declares, "NO PENALTY FOR YOU!" See Romans 8:1.

How is it possible for God to justify us, i.e., to simply set aside the penalty of eternal hell, which in all justice we deserve? Because Jesus died on the cross as our substitute, accepting the penalty of divine wrath in our place. We do not have to pay this penalty, because Jesus has paid it for us. So when God declares, "No penalty for you!", He is righteous or just in doing so because of the cross (Romans 3:26). I.e., Jesus's death on the cross is the BASIS or GROUND for our justification. This is the meaning of Romans 5:9.

The fact is that Jesus's atoning death actually paid the penalty for EVERY human being's sins, but not everyone receives the gracious gift of the cancellation of this debt, i.e., not everyone is actually justified. Why not? Because God has laid down specific conditions for receiving the gift. One of these conditions is the MEANS by which the gift is received, which is where faith comes in. God gives justification only to those who exercise "faith in his blood" (Romans 3:25). Faith is the empty hand with which the sinner must reach out and accept the gift. This is what it means to be "justified by faith" (Romans 3:28 and elsewhere).

To summarize, we are justified by the death of Christ as its BASIS, and we are also justified by faith as the MEANS by which we receive it.

I should also note that there are other *conditions* for receiving justification besides faith. When the Bible speaks of "justification by faith," it is specifying that faith is THE MEANS for receiving justification. But the New Testament also specifies that baptism is the OCCASION for receiving justification in this New Covenant age. "Means" is one kind of condition; "occasion" is another kind of condition. Many make the mistake of equating the concepts of means and conditions.

WHAT DOES 1 JOHN 1:9 MEAN?

QUESTION: You have said that a faulty understanding of 1 John 1:9 is a roadblock to a proper understanding of grace and a genuine sense of assurance. Please explain what 1 John 1:9 means.

ANSWER: I have done this in my book, *Set Free! What the Bible Says About Grace* (College Press, 2009; pp. 314-316). The following is from that source:

A main roadblock to assurance is a faulty understanding of 1 John 1:9. This familiar text reads, "If we confess our sins, He is faithful and righteous to forgive us our sins and to cleanse us from all unrighteousness." The typical approach to this text assumes that every time we commit a sin, we literally fall from grace. I.e., we lose our salvation status and re-enter the state of lostness. Even though all our previous sins remain forgiven, each time we sin again we become guilty for that sin and are condemned to hell for it, unless and until that sin can be forgiven. This is why 1 John 1:9 is so important, because (it is assumed) this text tells us how to get forgiveness for the sins we commit in our ongoing Christian life. If we sincerely confess that specific sin (and pray for its forgiveness), God will graciously forgive that sin and restore us to the saved state again—until we sin again, in which case the process must be repeated.

With this understanding of 1 John 1:9, a sincere Christian sees himself or herself as being trapped in a kind of revolving door between the domains of wrath and grace. The cycle is endless: under grace ⇨ sin ⇨

under wrath ⇨ confession ⇨ under grace ⇨ sin ⇨ under wrath ⇨ confession ⇨ under grace ⇨ sin ⇨ under wrath ⇨ confession ⇨ under grace – and on and on. How does this compromise assurance? Because it causes the Christian to live in fear that he or she will die after committing a sin and before having the inclination or opportunity to confess it and pray for forgiveness.

What is the solution to this life of fear and uncertainty? Of course, the simplest solution would be: just don't sin! But few of us (if any) are at this point. We still struggle with sin every day. Since that is the case, we need to see that the solution is: JUSTIFICATION BY FAITH! Committing a sin, in and of itself, does not separate us from the grace of God! We live our lives, day in and day out, performing good works and bad works (sins), while remaining under the gracious umbrella of justification through our faith in Jesus. Persistence in sin can cause our faith to die, but individual sins are not equivalent to apostasy. As someone has put it, those who are on a ship in the middle of the ocean can fall or jump off the ship and perish; but they can also trip and fall down on the ship, and thus hurt themselves, without falling off the ship. We are under grace, even when we sin.

Contributing to our faulty understanding of justification by faith and of 1 John 1:9 is a false teaching related to baptism, namely, the common idea that baptism is for the forgiveness of PAST SINS ONLY. This says that in baptism our past sins are forgiven like they are being erased from a blackboard; but after that, every time we sin, each new sin is added to the board until some subsequent ritual (such as the sacrament of penance, or the Lord's Supper, or the confession of 1 John 1:9) gets it erased. This is a seriously false understanding of baptism. Baptism is "for the forgiveness of sins" (Acts 2:38) because in that act we enter into an ongoing relationship with Jesus Christ, a relationship that is equivalent to being constantly covered by his blood just as the "robe of righteousness" (Isaiah 61:10) constantly covers our "filthy rags" (Isaiah 64:6). This covering remains secure unless we actually fall from grace by ceasing to believe in the atoning blood of Jesus.

What, then, does 1 John 1:9 mean? We learn this by looking at its context, especially the verses that precede and follow it: "If we say that we have no sin, we are deceiving ourselves and the truth is not in us.... If we say that we have not sinned, we make Him a liar and His word is not in us" (vv. 8, 10). The problem in both these verses is not sinning as such, but DENYING that we have sinned. What is the opposite of denying that we have sinned? Simply put, confessing that we HAVE sinned and ARE sinners. In my judgment this is the point of verse 9: if we confess that we ARE sinners, and in need of God's forgiveness, he is faithful to CONTINUE to keep us in the state of forgiveness. This is an element of our ongoing repentance. Even if we are not conscious of any recent specific sin, each time we pray we can still confess THAT we are sinners and claim anew God's promise of justification. (Confession of specific sins is still necessary for the sanctification process, though not for justification.)

This understanding of 1 John 1:8-10 is illustrated and confirmed by Jesus' parable of the Pharisee and the tax collector (Luke 18:9-14). The Pharisee is a perfect example of 1 John 1:8, 10; he was conscious only of his perceived goodness and admitted no sins at all. What about the tax collector? What specific sins did he confess? None! In simple humility he prayed, "God, be merciful to me, the sinner!" But he went home justified (forgiven), whereas the Pharisee did not.

SHOULD CHRISTIANS PRAY FOR FORGIVENESS?

QUESTION: I remember a conversation that came up in one of our classes in Bible college. Since Jesus has already died for our sins, do we ask for forgiveness in a prayer, or do we simply just thank God for having already forgiven us of our sins? Do we make a request, or just say, "Thank you"?

ANSWER: I will try to answer your question in several stages.

First, you would not say it this way: "Since Jesus has already died for our sins, do we ask etc.?" You would say it thus: "Since by God's grace we have already been justified through our faith in Jesus (i.e., since we have already received the gift of forgiveness), do we ask etc.?" The crucial point is not exactly that Jesus has already died for our sins, but that we have already received the benefit of that death in our baptism. As Christians we live in the state of forgiven-ness. It is not just our sins that are forgiven; we ourselves are forgiven *persons.*

Second, we continue in that state of forgiven-ness 24/7 by continuing to acknowledge our need for it and by continuing to trust in His saving death for us. We do not lose that forgiveness simply by committing a sin or sins (see below); we lose it by giving up our faith in Him.

Third, it is more precise to thank God for His ongoing gift of forgiveness than to ask Him for the gift. Acts 22:16 teaches that the sinner accepting Jesus for the first time should enter baptism praying for God to bestow the gift of forgiveness. Ananias exhorts Saul of Tarsus (later Paul the Apostle) thus: "Having arisen, and having called upon His name, get yourself baptized and wash away your sins." This is the literal translation. "Washing away sins" in this context is the same as forgiveness. "Calling on His name" (see Joel 2:32; Acts 2:21) is a prayer for forgiveness.

Fourth, it is perfectly appropriate to pray that God will CONTINUE to apply the atoning blood of Christ to us. Such a prayer is an ongoing acknowledgement of our sin and of our continuous need for forgiveness.

Fifth, a large element of this last prayer is praying that God would strengthen us to *keep our faith in Christ strong*, since our faith is what keeps us in the forgiven state.

Sixth, we do not lose our salvation each time we sin, thus do not need to utter a new prayer for forgiveness of that specific sin in order to be restored to the saved state. First John 1:9 is not talking about the confession of a specific sin in order to be forgiven again; it is talking about the ongoing confession THAT we are sinners as a condition for STAYING forgiven. (This is like an ongoing state of repentance.) This is in contrast with the person in 1 John 1:8,10, who DENIES THAT he is a sinner. In the parable of the Pharisee and the tax-collector, the Pharisee is the person in 1 John 1:8, 10; the tax-collector is the person in 1 John 1:9.

SUICIDE AND FORGIVENESS

QUESTION: If a Christian commits suicide, does he or she automatically go to hell? Doesn't the Bible say we must confess our sins in order for them to be forgiven? Surely suicide is a sin, but by its very nature it can be confessed only prior to the act. Is that sufficient in order to receive forgiveness for it?

ANSWER: We can certainly agree on some crucial points here: suicide (self-murder) is certainly a very serious sin, being a violation of the sixth commandment; committing any sin makes us guilty before God and worthy of hell; true repentance is definitely necessary as a condition for receiving forgiveness. When we put all these things together, it seems to require that anyone who commits suicide must go to hell. Is this conclusion Biblical?

It is commonly thought that the Roman Catholic Church takes this position, since it has traditionally denied a Catholic funeral and burial to anyone who has committed suicide. Recent Catholic writings have qualified this quite a bit, though. Some specifically say that the Catholic Church is more lenient on this today than it used to be. They acknowledge that the Church has a better understanding today of mental problems that may influence a suicide and thus affect personal responsibility. According to the *Catechism of the Catholic Church* (paragraphs 2282-83), "Grave psychological disturbances, anguish, or grave fear of hardship, suffering, or torture can diminish the responsibility of the one committing suicide.

We should not despair of the eternal salvation of persons who have taken their own lives. By ways known to him alone, God can provide the opportunity for salutary [saving] repentance." One Catholic author added this thought: "This qualification does not make suicide a right action in any circumstance; however, it does make us realize that the person may not be totally culpable for the action because of various circumstances or personal conditions" (William Saunders, "The Sin of Suicide," Catholic Education Resource Center, www.catholiceducation.org/en/culture/catholic-contributions/the-sin-of-suicide.html .)

While I deny the possibility of repentance after death (Hebrews 9:27), I believe the point about motivation is important for this issue. If suicide is an individual's act of defiance against God and a deliberate rejection of His Lordship, as an act of unbelief this may indeed separate the Christian from the grace of God and the hope of heaven. More commonly, though, the sin of suicide is actually an act of desperation and not a deliberate rebellion against God. As with most other specific sins, it does not automatically separate one from the grace of God, even if there have been no specific repentance and confession relating to it.

In many Protestant church circles, especially within the Restoration Movement, the view that underlies the question above—the idea that suicide automatically sends its perpetrator to hell—is based on a wrong approach to a specific passage of Scripture, namely, 1 John 1:9. In the NASB this reads, "If we confess our sins, He is faithful and righteous to forgive us our sins and to cleanse us from all unrighteousness." This is taken to mean that the act of repentant confession of a specific sin is required for the forgiveness of that sin, and it is assumed that this penitent act will take place after the sin has been committed—something that is impossible in the case of suicide.

In my judgment this is a faulty understanding of 1 John 1:9, and is the result of a failure to properly understand the key doctrine of justification by faith. According to this doctrine, we Christians who live with an ever-present, on-going attitude of faith and repentance, are in a constant *state* of forgiven-ness. We live as forgiven people, and we do so because of our faith in Jesus, apart from the record of our good works and our sins at any particular time (Romans 3:28). I have discussed this particular passage in my book on grace, *Set Free! What the Bible Says About Grace* (College Press, 2009), on pages 314-316.

Also, in a brief essay in this book you are now reading, just a few pages above, I have already quoted the six rather lengthy paragraphs from *Set Free!* that are relevant for this subject of suicide. I ask you to flip back a few pages and read that essay again. It is titled, "What Does 1 John 1:9 Mean?" I will wait while you go back and read that … .

… Assuming that you, my reader here, have now examined that material, I will make this final comment:

Any person who is contemplating committing suicide needs serious help; but if that person is a Christian, the false threat of guaranteed condemnation to hell is not the answer. If that sad act happens anyway, at least those of us who are left behind can grieve without being in despair over their eternal salvation.

PART FIVE

THE CHRISTIAN
WORLD VIEW

THE CHRISTIAN WORLD VIEW[1]

It may be an example of urban mythology, but reliable sources say it really happened. A philosophy examination at the University of Cincinnati once consisted of a single one-word question: "WHY?" One bright student boldly answered with only two words: "WHY NOT?" He got an A for the course.

Such an answer may be very witty, and it may even provide a surface satisfaction for an agnostic or atheistic mind. But sober reflection in general and Christian conviction in particular require us to seek a less flippant answer to the most basic questions of existence: What is this world all about? What IS this earth, this universe? Why do they exist at all? What does their history amount to? What is the meaning of it all?

The Christian answers to these questions stand in the sharpest contrast to those of the non-Christian. The difference can be summed up in the most basic of all antinomies, that between life and death. For the non-Christian, the watchword of the universe is *death*; but for the Christian, the key word is *life*. In this essay we shall attempt to set forth the Christian world view as it is revealed to us in Scripture. It is a story of life: life as created, life as destroyed by sin, life as recreated in resurrection from the dead.

I. THE WHY OF CREATION

In this section we are dealing with the question of origins, not only the whence but also the why. Our purpose is to show the great contrast between the Christian and non-Christian answers to questions such as those listed above.

A. The Non-Christian World View

First we must see how unbelievers answer questions concerning both the beginning and the end of the universe. What does the non-Christian have to say about the beginning of the universe? What can be its origin? Here modern man and modern science are significantly silent. They have absolutely no firm explanation for the origin of the materials from which the universe is made.

One attempt to solve this problem on a non-Christian basis was Fred Hoyle's "steady-state" or "continuous creation" theory, a view which he taught early in his career as an astronomer. This is the idea that all over the universe, hydrogen atoms are continuously popping into existence out of nothing at the rate of one atom per year in a volume about the size of a skyscraper. This surprisingly immense number of atoms then condenses to form new stars and galaxies.[2] Not surprisingly, scientific evidence itself eventually forced Mr. Hoyle to give up this theory.

Even if modern unbelievers cannot give a positive answer to the question of origins, the one thing about which they are absolutely certain is that things did not come from God. To Julian Huxley, for instance, "the idea that the universe must have been created, hence have a Creator, is scientifically old hat." He declared that the world "can now be accounted for in principle in naturalistic terms: to invoke the operation of God in the process is not only unnecessary but intellectually dubious."[3]

Since the non-Christian cannot explain the origin of the universe, the next best thing he can do is to explain its present order. To this question the unbeliever has a ready answer: what now is, is here by pure chance. As philosopher Bertrand Russell put it, "That man is the product of causes which had no prevision of the end they were achieving; that his origin, his growth, his hopes and fears, his loves and his beliefs, are but the outcome of accidental collocations of atoms ... are ... nearly certain."[4]

If things are the way they are because of chance or accident, then questions concerning the meaning and purpose of the universe are irrelevant. We begin to see the logic in answering the question "Why?" with a cynical "Why not?" As Hoyle says, "Here we are in this wholly fantastic Universe with scarcely a clue as to whether our existence has any real significance" (*Nature of the Universe*, 121). Concerning the universe, Huxley says, "Nowhere in all its vast extent is there any trace of purpose, or even of prospective significance. It is impelled from behind by blind physical forces, a gigantic and chaotic jazz dance of particles and radiations, in which the only over-all tendency we have so far been able to detect is ... the tendency to run down."[5]

Such a view of origins offers scant basis for any kind of hope for the future. Thus we are not surprised to see that the non-Christian's answer to the question of the end of the universe is eternal death. As Robert Frost puts it in his poem, "Fire and Ice,"[6]

> *Some say the world will end in fire,*
> *Some say in ice.*

This is the sum of two modern theories concerning the end of our earth and solar system. One theory is that the sun is getting hotter and hotter and will some day burn the earth's surface to a crisp. Men may try digging vast underground refrigerated caverns, but will not likely survive the great heat.[7] The other theory is that the sun is getting colder and colder; and one day it will simply "go out," and all life will freeze off the earth.[8] In either case, the ultimate end of our planet will be total death.

According to the generally accepted theory, though, whether our planet first fries or freezes, the final end of the whole universe will be eternal ice. No trace of life will remain. This prospect is based on the so-called second law of thermodynamics, or "the tendency to run down" which Huxley mentions above. In general terms this means that all the heat and energy now concentrated in small spaces in the universe (as in the sun) will one day be spread evenly through all of space, whence there is no returning again. It is like the color capsule in the first packages of white oleomargarine. Once you had spread it evenly throughout the margarine, there was no way to get it back into the capsule. In a similar way, once all the heat in the universe spreads evenly into the vast reaches of space between the stars and galaxies, it will remain there forever. The whole universe will then be the same freezing cold temperature.

As Gamow says, "Our sun will turn into a giant lump of lifeless matter covered with eternal ice and surrounded by a system of frozen but still faithful planets." By the year 10 billion A.D., infinite space will be sparsely filled with dead or dying stars (*Birth and Death of the Sun*, 159, 232). James Jeans agrees: "It matters little by what particular road this final state is reached; all roads lead to Rome, and the end of the journey cannot be other than universal death" (*The Mysterious Universe*, 15).

It is important to see that in such a view as this, the normal state of existence is death: eternal ice, not eternal life. Life is a fleeting exception, "an utterly insignificant fraction of the total activity of the material universe" (Jeans, 13). It is but "an exceptional state or aggregation of matter."[9] As one evolutionist put it, "Man ... and all other forms of life are evolutionary accidents."[10] Irving Adler has said that "the development of life appears as something that just *happened* without design or purpose. It started from the accidental mixing and combining of chemicals in the primitive sea."[11] This modern view is well described by Karl Heim:[12]

> The whole creation is like a wood, through which the forester has gone with axe in hand, marking with a stroke every tree which is to be felled in the approaching deforestation. So every man, however young and healthy he may be, is already marked for death, and has a precisely predetermined time still to live, before it is his turn in the universal death which pervades the whole creation.

There is no better expression of the unbeliever's hopeless pessimism than this statement by Bertrand Russell ("A Free Man's Worship," 47-48):

That all the labours of the ages, all the devotion, all the inspiration, all the noonday brightness of human genius, are destined to extinction in the vast death of the solar system, and that the whole temple of man's achievement must inevitably be buried beneath the debris of a universe in ruins—all these things, if not quite beyond dispute, are yet so nearly certain, that no philosophy which rejects them can hope to stand. Only within the scaffolding of these truths, only on the firm foundation of unyielding despair, can the soul's habitation henceforth be safely built.

Such is the non-Christian world view. The significant thing about it is that death is the eternal meaning and destiny of all things: not just a dead bird, or a dead cat, or even a dead man, but a dead universe (which corresponds nicely to the modern concept of a "dead God"). Death is all we have to look forward to. Death is the normal state. Life is abnormal; it is only here by accident and lasts for only a fleeting moment. It is an intruder which will soon vanish, and then all will become normal and dead again.

B. The Christian World View

How utterly opposed to the above is the Christian world view! The idea that death is the normal state and our inevitable fate is exactly the opposite of the Bible's teaching. The notion that life is an odd and fleeting intruder is directly contrary to God's word. For according to Scripture, *life* is the normal state, *life* is the watchword of the universe. Death is the abnormal state, the intruder, the usurper. For in the beginning, the living God created a living universe dominated by a living creature destined to eternal life.

The universe is not eternal matter arranged into its present order by accident. It is the purposeful creation of the living and eternal God, created from nothing by His almighty power. It is important to take note of the role of the eternal Son of God in the creation: "All things came into being by Him; and apart from Him nothing came into being that has come into being" (John 1:3). "For by Him all things were created, both in the heavens and on earth, visible and invisible, whether thrones or dominions or rulers or authorities—all things have been created by Him and for Him" (Colossians 1:16).

Since the universe has a definite origin, it also has a purpose. It *does* make sense to ask the question "Why?" of the creation as a whole. The ruling principle, the controlling purpose of the universe may be summed up, not in the word "death," but in the word "life."

Our concern, of course, is with our own planet. Whether there is or is not life elsewhere is beside the point for our present purpose, for life on this planet is all that the Bible is concerned with. (It is interesting, though, that no real evidence has been uncovered to establish the existence of life anywhere else in the universe.)

The fact of life is a dominant emphasis in the first chapters of Genesis. On the third day God created the vegetable kingdom, with all its abundant varieties of grass, herbs, and fruit trees (1:11-12). On the fifth and sixth days He created the animal kingdom, or "every living creature that moves" (1:20-25). Then on the sixth day God made the final living creature, man himself (1:26-27; 2:7). In the midst of His creation God placed the symbol of His purpose and plan for man and for the entire universe: the tree of *life* (2:9).

The very presence of life on our planet is a marvel which too often goes unappreciated. In this connection it is edifying to meditate on pictures of the moon's surface. What a contrast between its rocky, dusty barrenness and our living earth! Here the abundance and variety of living things stagger the imagination. Everywhere we go, we are surrounded by life: on the highest mountains, in the deepest oceans, in every nook and cranny of land, and even in the *Dead* Sea![13]

What is the purpose of these myriad forms of life? In God's original creation they were all made for the sake of and for the subservience of one of their own number: the living creature called man. The focus of all life is the life of the human race. Man is the crown and goal of creation; all the rest is *for man*, for man to subdue and to use. The plant and animal kingdoms sacrifice their life for the sustenance and comfort of the life of man. This is the creation order.

What makes man so important? Is not this view rather conceited? Why is the life of man more important than the life of a dog, or even of a roach? The answer is that man is the creature which is made in the image of the living God, and therefore the creature which may have fellowship with the Creator Himself and may worship and serve the Lord of all. In this statement we come to the purpose and goal of all creation: a living creature to serve and love and commune with the living God forever. Herein is summarized the Christian world view.

We confess then that life is the focus and purpose and meaning of this world. Life is the original and normal state. The goal of creation is man as a living creature, made in the image of God for the purpose of communion with God and service to God. This is truly a cause for hope and rejoicing, not "unyielding despair."

Is it any wonder that we Christians emphasize eternal life, not eternal ice? Is it any wonder that we are so concerned with the ravages of sin and death, which are the enemies of God and the very contradiction of His original purpose? Is it any wonder that we serve the risen Savior, Jesus Christ, who saw His own creation fall into this terrible condition, and came to die and rise again in order to restore and recreate everything in it, including us?

II. AN UPSIDE-DOWN WORLD

Read Genesis 1:31: "And God saw all that He had made, and behold, it was very good." Now read a book of any kind of history. Read about the great catastrophes of natural history, such as the eruptions of Mt. Vesuvius or the San Francisco earthquake. This is "very good"? Read about the atrocities of political history, such as the Babylonian and Roman destructions of Jerusalem, or the Nazis' attempted extermination of the Jews. This is "very good"? Read about the scandals of church history, such as the torture and hideous execution of countless so-called heretics at the hands of so-called Christian officials (both Catholic and Protestant). This is "very good"?

Clearly something has gone wrong. Surely the world that *is*, is not the world that God originally declared to be "very good." How true this is! God's pure and living and vibrant creation has been corrupted by sin and death. As a result things are far from normal, far from being "very good." In fact we may truly say that sin has turned the world *upside down*. How sin has thus affected the whole world order is the topic that will be discussed in this section.

A. A Description of the Fall

In order to see what happened in the fall of man or the upsetting of the creation order, we must first understand what this order was before the fall. In terms of rulership or authority, man (both male and female) originally stood midway between God and the rest of the earthly creation. He could rightly be called "king of the earth" and "servant of God."

God created man to be king of the earth,[14] as the very order of creation suggests. Man, the last creature to be brought into existence, is the crown of creation. Everything preceding his appearance is only preparation; it was created for man, *for* his use and enjoyment (1 Timothy 6:17). To this end God commanded the first couple to subdue the earth and have dominion over it, to bring "all the earth" under their control (Genesis 1:26-27; Psalms 8).

But man was created not only as king of the earth, but also as servant of God. He is the crown of creation, but he is still a creature. He is to subdue the earth, but he is to subdue it for God's glory. Whatever he brings under his control, he then must submit to the Lord of all.

The first transgression represents an attempt to break out of this God-ordained order. Not content with a position of authority midway between God on the one hand and the rest of the physical creation on the other hand, Adam and Eve tried to move up a notch. Not content with being servants of God, they desired to be equal with God and independent of His rule (Genesis 3:1-6).

The result, however, was just the opposite. In attempting to move up a notch, man instead slipped down a notch. Far from becoming equal with God, man is no longer even a blessed servant. His disobedience has made him a rebel against God, a cowardly rebel whose fear makes him desire to hide from God's presence (Genesis 3:8ff.). Furthermore, because of his desire for more authority, man has forfeited even the dominion that he originally had. He is no longer the king, but rather the slave of creation. The very earth that once served him is now his master and his foe (Genesis 3:17-19).

Thus we may say that the world has been turned upside down. The whole world order has been mightily upset. Man, the intended king of creation and servant of God, has become the slave of creation and a rebel against God. This is indeed a fall.

B.   The Dominion of Death

Nothing portrays the upside-down character of the world better than the role of death in the present order of things. As we saw in the previous section, the watchword of God's original creation was *life*. Death itself was an integral part of that creation, but its role was that of a servant. Members of the plant and animal kingdoms sacrificed their life for the sake of the life of man, their master.[15]

But now, after the entrance of sin, death is no longer the servant. Death is now the king of the universe; and man, the intended king, is forced to bow himself to the very dust before its sinister dominion (see Romans 5:14, 17).

Death was crowned king in the garden of Eden itself. Here is where death first entered the human realm, and it entered because of Adam's sin. "Through one man sin entered into the world, and death through sin" (Romans 5:12). The death that Adam suffered was two-fold. First, he suffered a spiritual death, or the death of his soul. The awakening of his sense of sin was accompanied by the deadening of his moral powers and the corruption of the image of God in which he was made. This happened the very moment he sinned, as God had promised (Genesis 2:17). Then, like the nocturnal creatures who flee from the source of light, Adam the death-dominated creature sought to hide from the source of life (Genesis 3:8).

But Adam's sin made him liable also to physical death, the death of his body. This did not happen immediately, but the rest of his life was lived under the ominous shadow of the knowledge of his mortality (Genesis 3:19). Adam, who came from the hand of God a living creature, was now a dying creature.

In some incomprehensible way, the sin of Adam has placed the entire human race under the dominion of death. Because of the sin of this one man, death reigns as king over us today (Romans 5:12-19).

Our death, like Adam's, is two-fold. First of all, there is death as a spiritual condition, the death of the soul. This death reigns within us even though we are very much "alive and kicking" from a physical standpoint (see 1 Timothy 5:6). We are, as Paul says, "dead in [our] trespasses and sins" (Ephesians 2:1; Colossians 2:13). As Alexander Campbell puts it, we are "greatly fallen and depraved in our whole moral constitution."[16] This is that condition of spiritual corruption which is so radical that its remedy can be described only in terms of rebirth, re-creation, and resurrection. What was true of the Prodigal Son is true of every converted sinner: "This son of mine was dead, and has come to life again" (Luke 15:24).

Spiritual death thus reigns in the hearts of man. Here is the reason why our history books and newspapers are filled with accounts of murder, hatred, and war. Here is the reason why there is so much sin in the world. Here is the reason why God's original pronouncement, "It was very good," does not apply to today's world.

But a second aspect of death also permeates the whole of the human race, namely, physical death as the penalty for sin. All human beings are truly dying creatures, caught up in the irreversible process that leads back to the dust. In view of this inevitable fate, even while it is alive now, Paul can say "the body is dead because of sin" (Romans 8:10).

Because of sin! Yes, death is the wages of sin (Romans 1:32; 6:23). It is the penalty prescribed by God upon all the children of Adam (Romans 5:12-19). Why do most people fear this death (Hebrews 2:15)? Because physical death is simply the threshold of the courtroom of the Righteous Judge (Hebrews 9:27), the one before whose eyes "all things are open and laid bare" (Hebrews 4:13). Physical death is the prelude to the Judgment Day, when Adam's offspring in their naked guilt will try to hide from the presence of the Lord (Revelation 6:16). Physical death, as bad as it is in itself, is also the symbolic foretaste of the final penalty meted out to unbelieving sinners, a penalty which is called the second death in the lake of fire that burns forever and ever (Revelation 20:10-15; 21:8).

Thus we see that death as the penalty for sin is not limited to physical death, but reaches its climax in the eternal death that is hell itself.

We speak of the dominion or lordship of death in the world, but death is actually only a puppet king who represents the one who actually reigns over this present evil age, the devil himself. The devil is the one who has the power of death (Hebrews 2:14). The devil is the prince of this world, the god of this age (John 12:31; 2 Corinthians 4:4). But he is only a pretender, a usurper who has no inherent right to that which he claims as his own. In other words, the fact that death and the devil reign in this world is a complete reversal of the created order. The world has been turned upside down.

C. Normal or Not?

According to Paul, even the non-rational creation feels the terrible burden of this abnormal situation and cries out to be delivered from its "slavery to corruption" (Romans 8:21; see vv. 18-22). But the tragic thing is that inanimate nature knows more about the real condition of things than most people do! The average person today is not aware that there is anything radically wrong with his world.

In view of the wretched condition of the world after the fall of Adam, it is incredible that anyone could say that everything is normal. Yet this is precisely the verdict pronounced by sinful man: all is normal. "Whatever is, is good." Certainly unbelievers acknowledge the presence of evils such as war, hatred, and death. But these things are only imperfections, defects, undesirable elements. They are regrettable and need to be eliminated, yet they are normal. According to the clean version of the old slang expression, everything is SNAFU: Situation Normal, All Fouled Up.

For over a century and a half, the doctrine of naturalistic evolution has supplied the unbeliever with a basis for this judgment. He sees the present world as the result of a long process of natural, undirected evolutionary development. This process has not been interrupted by any violent upheaval or reversal, such as the fall of Adam. In view of this steady progress, he asserts that the present stage is the best yet, though it is admittedly imperfect. Any defects are due to the fact that the process is incomplete; therefore they are a normal part of the system. And the most normal aspect of all is the all-pervasiveness of death!

Many years ago two college teams engaged in a radio debate concerning this proposition: "Man, all things considered, is a disappointment." That one team could deny this proposition is simply beyond belief; but it is typical of the modern world that even the team which affirmed it, giving as evidence the prevalence of war, poverty, and hatred, could still speak only in terms of "disappointment"! Not sin, not disgrace, not distortion—just disappointment.

This is how we want to think of ourselves. How many times have we tried to excuse our own sins on these very same grounds? "To err is human," we repeat. "Nobody's perfect. Everybody makes mistakes." And we reassure ourselves, "We live in modern times, and all's well. Every day, in every way, the world is getting better and better."

But into the midst of these empty excuses and hollow hopes comes the judgment of God: NO! The world is not normal! It has been turned upside down by man's rebellion. The world is standing on its head. The proper order of relationships has been wholly reversed.

It is the Christian's task to inform the complacent world that it is not normal, and that the root of this abnormality is sin. Such a story is unpleasant to tell and unflattering to hear, and by itself it would be a message of doom. But this is not the end of the message. To this we must add the good news of the death and resurrection of Christ, the means by which the upside-down world is set right side up again.

When Paul and Silas went to Thessalonica, they preached how "Christ had to suffer and rise again from the dead," and proclaimed Him as the Messiah or Savior of the world (Acts 17:3). Many conversions took place. In response the unbelieving enemies of the gospel cried out, "These that have turned the world upside down are come hither also" (Acts 17:6, KJV). Ironically enough, these rabble-rousers have accurately described the revolutionary results of the death and resurrection of Jesus, namely, a complete reversal of the present world order. But they were wrong in this respect: the world was already upside down as the consequence of sin and death. Jesus Christ died and rose again to conquer these usurpers, thereby restoring His own creation to its rightful condition.

III. A NEW BEGINNING

An indulgent father gives his eighteen-year-old son a new automobile. "It's yours," he says. "Take it. Use it wisely and enjoy it." But the very first time the eager young driver gets behind the wheel, he yields to the temptation to "see what it will do." As he speeds down the highway, he loses control, smashes the car, and kills himself. When the father is summoned to the scene, he can only weep helplessly. He is completely powerless to give his son life again.

Part of this tragic tale describes what has happened to the world that God made and gave to man. By his sin, man has made a total wreck of the world and has brought the condition and penalty of death upon himself.

The whole universe, including us today, wears the shroud of death. Death is our state, and death is our fate.

But unlike the helpless father in the story, our heavenly Father is not powerless in the face of death. The God who created the heavens and the earth need not and will not abandon His handiwork to the usurper, death. Instead He surveys the ruins of His old creation and declares that He will do something about it. He will deliver His creatures from the dominion of death; He will redeem His own from the bondage of corruption.

The world is so completely corrupt, however, that no minor repair job can restore it to its proper order. A thorough renovation is required. Therefore God has determined to make a new beginning, to bring forth a new order of things out of the old. He announces, in the most radical terms possible, that He will fashion a new creation. This promise is first given through the prophet Isaiah (65:17): "For behold, I create new heavens and a new earth; and the former things shall not be remembered or come to mind." It is repeated by Peter: "But according to His promise we are looking for new heavens and a new earth, in which righteousness dwells" (2 Peter 3:13). The final fulfillment of the promise is revealed to John in a vision: "And I saw a new heaven and a new earth; for the first heaven and the first earth passed away" (Revelation 21:1).

When does this new creation begin? Of course, we know that it will not be completed until after the Judgment Day as described by John. But it is important to see that the new creation has already begun, and that it is in existence even today. The new beginning occurred specifically in the resurrection of Jesus Christ from the dead, and the new creation exists today in the form of the church.

In this section we are concerned with the new beginning. Although we have designated the resurrection of Jesus as the precise beginning point, we cannot separate this event from the crucifixion. These are two inseparable aspects of the one redemptive work of Christ, both of which are aimed at overcoming the dominion of death.

A. The Penalty Is Paid

In the preceding section we pointed out how death reigns over God's original creation in a two-fold way. First, it exercises its tyranny as a spiritual state or condition; we are all "dead in ... trespasses and sins" (Ephesians 2:1). Also, we are all under the sentence of death as the penalty for sins (Romans 6:23). The penalty refers not only to physical death, but also and primarily to the eternal second death in the lake of fire (Revelation 21:8).

Let us consider this penalty for a moment. We can safely say that the eternal death described in Scripture is the worst penalty imaginable to a mortal mind; and no doubt its reality is worse than our conception of it. And this is only just, for sin against God is the worst crime imaginable. From the standpoint of pure justice, what punishment is deserved by the five "Hell's Angels" who raped a college girl and left her with the mentality of a five-year-old child? What punishment is deserved by the evil fiends who tortured a civil rights worker to death by methodically breaking every bone in his body? What penalty is bad enough for the murderers of Jesus Christ our Lord? Can we possibly imagine a penalty that is severe enough?

And yet every sin, as a violation of God's law, is a violation of the very nature of God. Just as the soldiers slapped Jesus, spit on Him, and finally killed Him, so do we spit in God's face, mock Him, and slap Him when we sin. To put it in its rawest form, sin is a rebellious attempt to kill God. What penalty, then, does our sin deserve? The worst possible one, not only in our imagination but in reality. And this is the one which God has decreed that we must suffer.

We can immediately see the problem involved regarding the new creation. All have sinned, and all therefore stand under the penalty of eternal death. Once this penalty is executed, it cannot be revoked. And God's justice demands that it be executed. What hope is there, then, for a new creation, if all men are condemned to eternal death? What hope is there for you and me, who face this very fate?

At this moment of seeming hopelessness, God reveals Himself not only as Power and Justice, but also as Wisdom and Love. For the very God who imposed the sentence of death upon His sinful creatures has taken this same penalty upon Himself and has paid it in full. He is like the just judge who sentences his friend to death in the electric chair, then sits in the chair himself. This is in effect what Jesus Christ, the incarnate Word, has done for us on the cross. In His crucifixion Jesus died not just an ordinary human physical death. This is impossible for one who has not sinned, and for one who is God Himself. In His death Jesus the Lord of Glory suffered the equivalent of the death specified in the penalty; He endured agony equal to an eternity in hell for every person. No wonder He recoiled in Gethsemane!

This is what happened on Calvary. This is what it means to say "Christ died for our sins." It means that He took upon Himself the penalty which we ourselves deserve, "having become a curse for us" (Galatians 3:13), and being "made ... to be sin on our behalf" (2 Corinthians 5:21). For us! On our behalf!

By paying the penalty for sin with His own death on the cross, Jesus redeems His old creation and prepares the way for the new.

B. The Tyrant Is Defeated

The saving work of Christ does not end with the cross, however. Although the penalty for sin is thereby paid, death like a tyrant still holds mankind in its power both physically and spiritually. Though the sting of death is gone (see 1 Corinthians 15:56), the death of the body is inescapable. Also, the soul of man is still dead in trespasses and sins. Therefore Christ's redemptive mission can be completed only when He rises from the dead and thereby breaks the power of death once and for all.

In order to picture how the resurrection of Jesus Christ has overthrown the tyrant Death, let us imagine an allegorical setting. Let us consider all of God's original creation to be imprisoned, as it were, in a great dungeon, which represents death. In Biblical terms, the dungeon may be called Hades, which is the place of death. Every child of Adam is a prisoner in this dungeon, and Satan himself as its keeper gleefully guards the keys.

The Bible describes the work of Christ as a confrontation with and victory over death and the devil. Jesus Himself declared that He came "to give His life a ransom for many" (Mark 10:45). A ransom implies rescue from bondage. John tells us, "The Son of God appeared for this purpose, that He might destroy the works of the devil" (1 John 3:8). The clearest statement of all is in Hebrews 2:14, which says that the Son of God took upon Himself mortal flesh and blood, "that through death He might render powerless him who had the power of death, that is, the devil."

Thus to engage in conflict with the keeper of the keys of death was one reason why Jesus came. Throughout His ministry He fought and won many preliminary skirmishes, as at His temptation and in His casting out of demons. But the major battle was staged on Calvary and at the garden tomb. Shortly before it occurred Jesus Himself described it as the decisive conflict: "Now judgment is upon this world; now the ruler of this world shall be cast out.... The ruler of the world is coming, and he has nothing in Me.... The ruler of this world has been judged" (John 12:31; 14:30; 16:11).

Then on Calvary it happens. The Son of God wrestles in mortal combat with the one who guards the dungeon of death—and is defeated! Yes, Jesus Himself is apparently overcome by the evil one, and is cast into the dungeon of death! How can it be? Will the gates of Hades after all prevail?

No! For in his struggle with the Son of God, the keeper of the dungeon spends all his strength and falls powerless. The serpent's head at last has been crushed (Genesis 3:15). And then the incredible happens. Jesus had been crucified and killed, "but God raised him to life again, setting him free from the pangs of death, because it could not be that death should keep him in its grip" (Acts 2:24, NEB). In triumph Jesus breaks forth from the dungeon of death. "Death could not keep its prey; He tore the bars away!" Then, snatching up the keys from the fallen keeper, He holds then high and says, "I am the Living One; I was dead, and behold I am alive for ever and ever! And I hold the keys of death and Hades" (Revelation 1:18, NIV).

Thus is the tyrant defeated through the resurrection of Jesus Christ. "We know that Christ, once raised from the dead, is never to die again: he is no longer under the dominion of death" (Romans 6:9, NEB). "For he has broken the power of death and brought life and immortality to light through the Gospel" (2 Timothy 1:10, NEB).

C. The Foundation Is Laid

Colossians 1:18 says of Jesus that "He is also head of the body, the church; and He is the beginning, the firstborn from the dead." That is to say, the resurrection of Jesus marks the beginning of the new creation. It is the basis for a new order of things, a universe once again characterized by life, a world in which death no longer reigns (Revelation 21:4).

The resurrection of our Lord is both the foundation and the guarantee of the new creation. Regarding the former, let us now consider the old creation not as imprisoned in a dungeon but as a building that has been destroyed. When it first came from the hand of its builder, it was beautiful indeed. But now it lies in ruins, its once-glorious wood and stone reduced to a pile of splinters and chips. Then in the fulness of time the original builder comes to the very site of the ruins in order to start all over again. When his work is finished, there appears amidst the heap of rubble a new and firm foundation laid upon solid rock. This unshakable foundation is our risen Lord Himself.

This is to say that the resurrection of Jesus is not only the *first* permanent resurrection from the dead; it is also the resurrection upon which all future resurrections rest. His is the life upon which all life now depends. From our risen Christ emanates "the power of an indestructible life" (Hebrews 7:16), a power that infuses new life into our bodies and souls and sustains the living church in the midst of a dying world. The church's one foundation is Christ her risen Lord.

Jesus's resurrection is not only the foundation but also the guarantee of the new creation. This is why Paul calls Jesus the firstfruits of the dead (1 Corinthians 15:20, 23). The firstfruits are the guarantee of further harvest, in this case of further resurrections. The redeemed will be "conformed to the image of His son, that He might be the first-born among many brethren" (Romans 8:29). In this respect Jesus is the second and last Adam (1 Corinthians 15:45, 47), the head and beginning of a new family.

The resurrection of Jesus Christ is the foundation and guarantee of our own personal rebirth, our own personal deliverance from the dungeon of death. God has promised to make new creatures out of us if we come to Christ (2 Corinthians 5:17), and Christ's resurrection confirms this promise. The God of power who raised Jesus from the dead can give us life, too (Ephesians 1:18-25). Christ is the resurrection and the life; if we believe on Him we shall live forever (John 11:25-26). If we believe that God raised Jesus from the dead (Romans 10:9), and if we trust in this resurrection as we submit to baptism (Colossians 2:12; 1 Peter 3:21), we shall be saved. We, too, shall know "the power of His resurrection" (Philippians 3:10)!

IV. THE NEW CREATION

Because of His resurrection from the dead, Jesus is called the firstborn from the dead, the firstborn among many brethren, the firstfruits of them that sleep (Colossians 1:18; Romans 8:29; 1 Corinthians 15:20). He is the *first* because His resurrection is only the beginning of a whole new order of things. In this one pre-eminent display of the life-giving power of God, the new creation is inaugurated.

What is this new creation? How are we related to it? These are the questions to be answered in this section.

A. The Church

In this essay we have summed up God's purpose for his original creation with the word "life." We have seen how this purpose was interrupted when death gained dominion over the world through Adam's sin. We have also seen how Jesus Christ came to deal with death and to bring life and immortality to light through His own death and resurrection. In so doing He established a new order of existence from which death is excluded and in which God's original purpose for His creatures is renewed. In other words, He has begun a new creation in which *life* is once more the watchword.

At this present time, the new creation is the church, as the familiar hymn says, "The church's one foundation is Jesus Christ her Lord; she is His new creation by water and the word." That the church is God's new kingdom of life is indicated by Jesus in His exchange with Simon Peter at Caesarea Philippi. When Peter confessed Jesus to be the Christ, the Son of God, he heard Jesus reply, "On this rock I will build my church, and the forces of death shall never overpower it" (Matthew 16:18, NEB). Here is what Jesus came to do, and He is doing it still today. He is building a living church that shall forever be free from the curse and corruption of death.

From what is this church constructed? Peter himself tells us when he describes the church as a spiritual temple which is built from "living stones" (1 Peter 2:5). He means that the church is made up of men and women who are spiritually alive. But all sinners under the curse of the old creation are *dead* in trespasses and sins (Ephesians 2:1); they are all under the penalty and power of death. Where then can "living stones" be found? Where among this rubble-heap can the Master Builder find anything suitable for His new and living creation?

Let us not forget that Christ the risen Lord has the keys to death and Hades (Revelation 1:18), and thus can release us lifeless stones from the power of death. Even though we are dead in trespasses and sins, God can make us alive with Jesus Christ (Ephesians 2:1-5). He can make new creatures out of those who are broken and useless (2 Corinthians 5:17). He can take us who are lifeless pieces of rubble and fashion us anew with His life-giving power so that we are fit to be built into His living church.

This redeeming process can be described only as a resurrection from the dead.

B. The Resurrection of Our Dead Souls

How does one become a part of this new creation? What must we do to have Christ remake us and give us life? The answer is that Christ will raise our souls from spiritual death when we are willing to say to Him with deepest conviction,

> *Have thine own way, Lord; have thine own way;*
> *Thou art the Potter, I am the clay.*
> *Hold me and make me after Thy will,*
> *while I am waiting, yielded and still.*

Here is the answer: absolute surrender to Christ, the living One. This is what it means to believe on the Lord Jesus Christ (Acts 16:31). We truly believe when we unhesitatingly accept the testimony about His life, death, and resurrection; when we confidently trust in His promises and His ability to fulfill them; when we yield ourselves, body and soul, to His resurrecting power; and when we totally commit ourselves to His will for us.

The resurrection of Jesus is a specific object of our faith and trust. We must believe that Jesus was actually raised from the dead. "If you confess with your mouth Jesus as Lord, and believe in your heart that God raised Him from the dead, you shall be saved" (Romans 10:9). We must also believe in His power to raise us from death. Jesus said, "I am the resurrection and the life; he who believes in Me shall live even if he dies, and everyone who lives and believes in Me shall never die" (John 11:25-26). Our sins shall be forgiven if we "believe in Him who raised Jesus our Lord from the dead" (Romans 4:24).

If we have this confidence and this trust in the resurrection of Jesus, He will raise us from the dead also. At this point the focus is upon a resurrection that takes place within us, a resurrection of our dead souls. This is God's remedy for that spiritual and moral death which holds sway over us. We cannot conquer it ourselves; but when we yield ourselves to God, He makes us alive again. The Bible calls this an act of renewal or regeneration or being born again.

It is proper to ask when this resurrection of our dead souls occurs. The Bible indicates that it happens in the moment we consummate our surrender to Christ in the act of baptism. It is here that we become recipients of the saving work of God through Jesus Christ, "having been buried with Him in baptism, in which you were also raised up with Him through faith in the working of God, who raised Him from the dead" (Colossians 2:12).

This passage of Scripture tells us part of what is going on during the act of baptism: nothing less than a resurrection from the dead. The person being baptized is undergoing an operation on his soul, an operation that Paul describes in Colossians 2:11 as a spiritual circumcision, "a circumcision made without hands." Then he adds, "And although you were dead because of your sins and because you were morally uncircumcised, he has made you alive with Christ" (Colossians 2:13, NEB).

This passage also shows us that faith is still the main emphasis and the decisive factor in the new birth, even during the act of baptism. For the resurrection of our dead souls occurs here only "through faith in the working of God." In other words, baptism is effective only when we submit to it in sincere faith that God is doing something here to save us from our sins. We do not trust in the water or in the one who is baptizing us. Instead we put our trust solely in the life-giving power of God, believing that just as surely as we are buried into and raised up out of the water, so is God raising our soul up out of the grave of spiritual death.

But how do we know this is happening to us? How can we be sure? Is there a sharp pain, a pleasurable sensation, a bright light, an inner voice, or some kind of physical change which assures us that God is so working within us? No, we do not need evidence of this kind. Instead, our assurance that God is raising us from spiritual death in baptism is grounded on the fact of the resurrection of Jesus Christ from the dead. In baptism we are raised to life with Christ through our faith in the working of God, the very same God who raised Jesus Himself from the dead (Colossians 2:12). The resurrection of Christ is thus the foundation of our faith that God can give life to our dead souls. The power He displayed in raising Christ is the means or the power He exerts upon us (Ephesians 1:19-20). Thus Peter can say that "baptism now saves you ... through the resurrection of Jesus Christ (1 Peter 3:21).

We must not lose sight of the significance of baptism, nor of its inseparable connection with faith, nor of the power of Christ's resurrection that makes it effective. The act of baptism is the act of trusting surrender in which Christ raises our dead souls to life. This is how He makes us into living stones and adds us to His new creation, the church.

C. The Resurrection of Our Dead Bodies

The new creation of God exists today as the group of persons who have been spiritually renewed by this inward resurrection in baptism. The evangelistic task of the church is to warn others of their dead condition and to show them the resurrecting power of Christ. Thus the church will continue to grow as more and more living stones are added to it.

But even though we have already experienced spiritual resurrection, the new creation will not be complete until our bodies have also been raised from the dead. Our hope of eternal life embraces not only our souls, but our bodies as well (Romans 8:23). Since our present mortal bodies have already signed an unbreakable covenant with death, salvation for them can only be in the form of resurrection from the dead (unless we are still alive at the second coming of Christ, 1 Corinthians 15:51-52).

That our bodies will be raised from the dead is a promise with a double guarantee. First of all, we know that our bodies will rise again because Jesus Himself has already been raised. "We know that the one who raised the Lord Jesus from the dead will also raise us with Jesus and present us with you in his presence" (2 Corinthians 4:14, NIV). Our bodily resurrection is just as certain as the resurrection of Jesus (1 Corinthians

15:12-22). Thus our Lord's resurrection is not only the ground of assurance concerning our spiritual resurrection in baptism, but it is also the basis of our confident hope in our future bodily resurrection as well (Romans 8:11).

The second guarantee of our bodily resurrection is the presence of the Holy Spirit within us. The giving of the Spirit is in fact the means by which spiritual life is infused into us at baptism (John 7:37-39; Acts 2:38). Our resurrection from spiritual death is accomplished by the gift of the Holy Spirit, and our continued life is sustained by His constant presence within us (1 Corinthians 6:19). But that's not the whole story: according to Scripture the presence of the Spirit in us now is God's pledge that He will one day raise our bodies from the dead (2 Corinthians 5:1-4). Since the presence of the Spirit is the means of our own spiritual resurrection, we may say that the fact that God has raised our souls from the dead assures us that He will raise our bodies also.

These two guarantees are joined together in Romans 8:11: "But if the Spirit of Him who raised Jesus from the dead dwells in you, He who raised Christ Jesus from the dead will also give life to your mortal bodies through His Spirit who indwells you."

What will this new body be like? We will have to wait for the resurrection itself in order to answer this in any detail. But even if we knew nothing at all about it, our hope could rest firmly and joyfully upon the fact of Christ's resurrection, for He "will transform the body of our humble state into conformity with the body of His glory, by the exertion of the power that He has even to subject all things to Himself" (Philippians 3:21).

We do know, though, that it will be different from the present body in many ways. It will no longer be susceptible to sickness, pain, or death. It will no longer make us embarrassed or frustrated by its weaknesses and limitations. It will be a spiritual body, but this does not mean it will be ghost-like or vapor-like. It means that the body itself will then be completely under the control of the Holy Spirit, and will be suited to an environment in which the Spirit reigns completely. See 1 Corinthians 15:42-44.

We can safely say also that the new body will be the same as this one in many respects. The person is the same, whether the body be old or new. As we might say to one of our friends who has lost a great deal of weight or has had her hair rearranged, "Oh, you look so *different!*" But we still know it is the same person.

The relation between our present body and our resurrection body may perhaps be like that between a seed and the flower which grows from it. There is a definite continuity between them; yet one is suited for the soil while the other is made to enjoy light and air. So will there be continuity between our old and new bodies, yet the new one will be suited to its new environment.

The Bible gives some hints that this new environment will resemble the old one in many ways. The present order of creation groans for its own deliverance (Romans 8:18-22), and Acts 3:21 speaks of the "restoration" of all things. Second Peter 3:10-13 describes the great burning of the universe, but this will probably be an act of purification and transformation rather than annihilation. We are promised a new *heavens* and a new *earth* (2 Peter 3:13), i.e., a new universe. What will its purpose be? It seems likely that our new bodies will dwell on the new earth, and that the new earth will bear some similarities to this present one. This seems so because upon that new earth will grow the tree of life, and over it will flow the water of life (Revelation 22:1-3). Thus in the very last chapter of the Bible we see God's original life-purpose for His creatures fulfilled in the new creation.

ENDNOTES

[1] This was first printed in the *Christian Standard*, March 30, April 6, 13, 20, 1968. It is used here by permission.

[2] Fred Hoyle, *The Nature of the Universe* (New York: New American Library, 1960), 106ff.

[3] *TIME* Magazine, August 1, 1960.

[4] Bertrand Russell, "A Free Man's Worship," in *Mysticism and Logic* (London: Longmans, Green and Co., 1919), 47-48.

[5] Julian Huxley, *Evolution in Action* (New York: New American Library, 1953), 11.

[6] Robert Frost, "Fire and Ice," in *The Poetry of Robert Frost*, ed. Edward Lathem (New York: Holt, Rinehart & Winston, 1969), 220.

[7] George Gamow, *The Birth and Death of the Sun* (New York: Viking Press, 1953), 118-121.

[8] James Jeans, *The Mysterious Universe* (New York: Macmillan, 1944), 15.

[9] C. B. Worth & Robert K. Enders, *The Nature of Living Things* (Signet Science Library, 1955), 8.

[10] Theodosius Dobzhansky, quoted in *Christian Standard* (Jan. 16, 1965), 4.

[11] Quoted in *Christian Standard* (Jan. 16, 1965), 4.

[12] Karl Heim, *The World: Its Creation and Consummation* (Edinburgh: Oliver and Boyd, 1962), 100.

[13] Gordon Gaskill, "The Dead Sea Isn't Dead Anymore," *Reader's Digest* (July 1966), 157ff.

[14] See Erich Sauer's book, *The King of the Earth* (Grand Rapids: Eerdmans, 1962).

[15] I owe this idea to Dr. Meredith Kline, one of my Old Testament professors at Westminster Theological Seminary.

[16] Alexander Campbell, *The Christian System* (Nashville: Gospel Advocate, 1974 reprint), chapter 7.

ABOUT THE AUTHOR*

(Photo collage - left to right/top to bottom)

1. **CRA Trustees 2013** – (Back Row) Jim Nichols (former CBI Director), Danny Dodds, Terry Peer, David Frye, Tom Claibourne, Russell James, Steve Henderson, (Front Row) Lee Mason, Jack Cottrell, Harvey C. Bream, Jr., and Paul Nichols.

2. Aaron Welch, former CBS Student and current faculty member at Central Christian College of the Bible wrote the following about Dr. Cottrell – *"I could not be more grateful for all I've learned from him over the years, especially his 'Doctrine of Grace' class which truly changed my life. I have so much respect for his lifetime of service."*

3. Dan Garrett - *"As the youth minister at White Oak Christian Church when we were members there early in my teaching career, Dan Garrett had very good influence on our children."*

4. *"One of my early students from the Great Northwest, Mike Kennedy is currently the preacher at the Minnehaha Church of Christ in Vancouver, WA."*

5. *"Mary and Walter Maxey, long-time missionaries in Japan, were among my earliest students."* Maxeys are pictured here with Jack and Barbara Cottrell. (Photo taken September 3, 2017)

6. Jack Cottrell, Johnny Pressley, and Michael Shannon speakers at the Florida Bible Conference, Kissimmee, Florida, January 2018. *"Two of my all-time favorite co-workers and Christian brothers!"*

7. Denver Sizemore, Men's Fellowship, Atlanta, GA circa 1984/1985 *"I think this was my only contact with Brother Sizemore. Wish I could have known him better!"*

---

*Dr. Cottrell provided some of the commentary on this collage.

THE COLLECTED WRITINGS OF JACK COTTRELL

Proudly made available by
The Christian Restoration Association
www.theCRA.org

Made in the USA
Monee, IL
04 November 2020